8‑2‑t

MW01617388

Not Just Small Change

Fund Development for Early Childhood Programs

Roberta L. Bergman

ISBN 978-0-942702-51-4

© 2010 Roberta L. Bergman. All rights reserved.

Published by:
Exchange Press
PO Box 3249
Redmond, WA 98073-3249
(800) 221-2864
www.ChildCareExchange.com

Cover Design: Scott Bilstad

All rights reserved. No part of this publication may be reproduced, stored in a retrieval system, or transmitted in any form by any means, electronic or mechanical, without prior written permission of the publisher.

TABLE OF CONTENTS

FOREWORD

This book summarizes most of what I have learned — as a professional and a volunteer, as an executive and a board member, as an advocate and a donor — about finding money to support organizations working with young children, their families, their caregivers, and their teachers.

I learned early on that it would never be sufficient to simply design or deliver programs. I'd have to justify the need, explain the solution, analyze public policy, convince funders, educate corporate executives, testify at hearings, write letters to the editor . . . and, often, it would still not be enough. Sometimes it seemed like life would be easier if I ran a book store. If someone wanted to buy a book, they'd buy a book. If they didn't want to buy a book, they wouldn't buy a book. There'd be no cajoling, convincing, advocating, phone calling, traveling to Washington, DC or the state capitol. Of course, look what has happened to independent book stores!

It's particularly gratifying that, after a long career that started at about the same time as policymakers began allocating limited funds for Head Start and child care, I now hear business leaders, governors, senators, and presidents making the case for increased money for early childhood programs. The old clichés are gone. I no longer hear "let's not encourage women to go to work by subsidizing their child care" — even though, deep down, I wish it were possible for more mothers to stay at home while their children are babies. Nor do I still hear "anyone can take care of children . . . women have been doing it since the dawn of time . . . why do caregivers need special training?" I'm sure there are some who continue to voice these objections, but they are not nearly as frequent or loud as before.

While I have benefited from the wisdom, experience, guidance, and colleagueship of countless people who have demonstrated unwavering commitment to young children, there are some who deserve special recognition.

◆ The late Dr. James L. Hymes was my most influential teacher. As the head of what was then a very small department of Early Childhood Education at the University of Maryland and a true leader in the field (he was one of the movers and shakers in the organization that later became the National Association for the Education of Young Children), he was literally years ahead of his time in voicing the importance of children's early experiences. His calm, measured tones and his down-to-earth style of writing made it seem that his thoughts were the most logical, sensible ideas in the world — and they were.

◆ As a young mother involved in the parent cooperative nursery school movement, I met parents — mostly professionals in other fields — who contributed their time, energy, and money to create high quality early childhood programs for their own children and those who would benefit in years to come. Parents in co-ops learned about children as they observed the range of developmental differences in groups of three- or four-year-olds. Co-ops built community. The co-op membership served as the extended family — particularly in times of need — for parents who lived far from their own kith and kin. And they fostered friendships that lasted for years.

◆ My friends and former co-workers at ChildCareGroup in Dallas — some now gone, some still hanging in there — became a significant part of my life when my family and I relocated to Texas. This agency is not only one of the oldest child care organizations in the nation, it is recognized for its exemplary model of Relationship-Centered Child Care® that provides high quality early childhood education in family-like environments. I am very proud to have played a role in this organization's growth, and I hope it keeps going strong for at least another 100 years.

◆ As a founding board member of the National Association of Child Care Resource and Referral Agencies (NACCRRA), I worked with some of the smartest, most articulate, and persuasive child care advocates in the country. These individuals made things happen — in their own communities and at the national level. Most of us were cut from the same cloth, but we all wore it differently. It has been a rewarding experience to watch NACCRRA grow from its early 'pass the hat to pay for postage' days to its established presence in Washington today.

◆ All that I learned as an Early Childhood major in college was put to the test with the arrival of my own four children — Elizabeth, Andrea, Michael, and Stephanie. They have grown into terrific, productive adults who are all blessed with a positive outlook, great sense of humor, generous spirit, and good jobs. I would quickly claim my daughter-in-law, Karin, and son-in-law, Jorge, as my own children if their families would allow it. And then there are the grandchildren — Zoe, Zachary, Sarah, Olivia, and Rachel — the precious embodiment of the ages and stages of early childhood.

◆ Finally, a word about my wonderful husband, Howard. He encouraged me to follow new paths at a time when I knew I wanted to work with children, but had no real career aspirations and not much self-confidence. When, as a newlywed, he decided to pursue a master's degree, he urged me to enroll in graduate school rather than spending my evenings alone while he was in class. When our second child was born during semester break prior to my last courses for my master's degree, he stood in long lines during the (pre-electronic) registration process to sign me up for the classes I needed. When, after a break in employment, I was offered a job that paid less than what I had previously earned in a similar position, he advised me to decline, even though there was no other job in sight (the offer was subsequently increased and I accepted the position). These may seem like insignificant acts, but they spurred my personal and professional growth, and I will always be grateful.

September 2009

ABOUT THE AUTHOR

Roberta L. Bergman is an experienced grant writer and consultant to non-profit organizations and has presented numerous workshops and seminars on grant writing, fundraising, marketing, and strategic planning.

She has worked on behalf of the children of Maryland, Ohio, and Texas. During her tenure as Senior Vice President of ChildCareGroup in Dallas, she secured over $300 million in grants, contracts, and contributions from public and private funding sources, and was frequently called upon by local and national media as an expert on child care issues.

Roberta holds a bachelor of science degree with high honors from the University of Maryland, where she majored in early childhood education. Her master's degree in educational administration and supervision is also from the University of Maryland.

INTRODUCTION

So You Need
to
Raise Money

Meeting the Need by Meeting the Challenge

The Oakton Infant, Toddler, and Parent Center was started by members of a local church as a free, part-time program to teach young mothers living in nearby public housing how to promote their children's early learning.

Administered by a small board of directors, staffed by volunteers, occupying an unused room in the church, and using supplies donated by church members, the program was soon at capacity, as more and more families learned about the difference it was making.

Three years after the program began, an electronics company announced plans to build an assembly plant in the area, spurred by tax incentives tied to hiring the housing project's residents. However, this new opportunity for the tenants to find suitable work seemed to be an empty promise in the absence of child care. Meanwhile, the waiting list at the center continued to lengthen.

The board members began to realize that the center could fold the current program into one which would meet this emerging need by enlarging its space, extending its hours, hiring a director and other paid staff, purchasing its own equipment and supplies, and transitioning from makeshift to market-driven. But although the market was growing, it consisted primarily of low-income families who could not pay the full cost of an expanded early childhood center.

Could the center raise the money to build and equip its own facility? Would it find the dollars to pay staff, year after year? Could it tap the generosity of the larger community? Were there foundations and corporations it could ask to help? Was there government funding the center could apply for?

The answer to these questions is, of course, "yes."

The challenge was learning how to do it.

What You Will Learn from this Book

This book is intended to help early childhood programs (preschools, child care centers, Head Start programs, etc.) and related organizations (resource and referral agencies, USDA Child and Adult Care Food Program sponsors, parent education groups, teacher training institutions, professional membership associations, and others) improve their capacity to bring in dollars from individual donations, corporate contributions, foundation grants, and government awards. Donations, contributions, and foundation grants are limited to non-profit organizations, although for-profit entities are often eligible to apply for government funding.

The terms 'center', 'program', 'agency', and 'organization' will be used interchangeably throughout the text to cover the range of entities which might raise money to benefit children and their families. These terms are not meant to exclude any specific entity nor differentiate between those that work with children and families directly (for example, a child care center) or indirectly (an early childhood advocacy organization). The principles, strategies, considerations, and suggestions are the same.

The book covers fundraising approaches that result in donations to support program operations, as well as gifts and grants for special purposes. It does not discuss 'PTA-type' fundraisers — bake sales, sales of candy or other pre-packaged merchandise, magazine subscription drives, or supermarket reward cards linked to charitable organizations. These efforts are simple to carry out, but they don't yield the kind of money that most organizations serving children need in order to sustain, expand, or improve their work. Just ask the Girl Scouts if their popular cookies produce enough dough.

- Chapter 1 lays the groundwork: the keys to raising funds for young children's programs, the fund development plan, and fundraising roles within an organization.

- Chapter 2 discusses how to identify potential donors or prospects, those who are familiar with your work and those who haven't a clue that your program exists.

- Chapter 3 covers strategies for asking prospects for money in face-to-face meetings or by telephone.

- Chapter 4 explores fundraising events, direct mail, and online donations.

- Chapter 5 examines grant-writing basics — finding grant sources, building relationships with them, and what needs to be in place before you write a proposal.

- Chapter 6 offers detailed guidance in writing foundation proposals — not only what should be included, but also how it should be presented.

- Chapter 7 delves into government grants, with specific examples of an Early Head Start application that can serve as a model for other public funding proposals.

- Chapter 8 covers the elements of capital campaigns.

- Chapter 9 is focused on 'writing to win,' including specific suggestions and excerpts from actual proposals that you can try your hand at re-writing.

- Chapter 10 suggests resources to aid in your quest for funding.

Read the whole book. Information presented in one chapter often applies to strategies covered in the others. Although processes, approaches, content, style, and formats will vary from one funding vehicle to another, they each have a common purpose: to bring new dollars into your organization to enable you to better serve children and families.

CHAPTER 1

Getting Started

The Key to Raising Money for Young Children's Programs

Young children are naturally appealing. Who can resist a baby cooing in her caregiver's arms? Or a toddler busily digging in the dirt, a three-year-old 'reading' his favorite book, a five-year-old explaining the architecture of the castle she has just constructed out of blocks? Who wouldn't want to help a little child grow and learn?

Interest in children goes beyond the individual who writes a check to your organization. Children's issues are gaining momentum on the national level. For example, an esteemed group of retired military leaders is calling for investments in early childhood education in order to preserve our nation's security, freedom, and opportunity. The Mission Readiness: Military Leaders for Kids 2009 report "Ready, Willing, and Unable to Serve" addresses the fact that 75% of today's 17 to 24 year olds do not meet the basic minimum standards required for military service. Mission Readiness states: "The path to success does not begin at age 17. The earliest months and years of life are a crucial time when we build the foundation of children's character, how they relate to others, and how they learn." Among the organization's recommendations: fully funding early childhood programs, supporting families in ways that improve parenting skills and reduce child abuse, and improving child health, mental health, and nutrition services.

The recognition by generals and admirals that high quality early childhood programs are vital to the future defense of our nation, coupled with widely-publicized research on brain development, the rapid growth of public pre-kindergarten programs, and debates on the federal government's role in education have increased awareness of the importance in helping children get off to the best start. Moreover, a 2004 survey conducted by the Advertising Council revealed that twice as many Americans (46%) had a positive view of children than in 1995 (23%). Almost everyone surveyed (97%) believed that one person can make a difference in the life of a child, and the majority (78%) indicated willingness to help. Even more interesting, the survey found few significant differences among demographic subgroups. Levels of involvement or willingness to get involved were not related to people's age, employment status, ethnicity, education, or income levels. This suggests that Americans are more united on children's issues than on many others — very good news for the early childhood profession.

Whether you work in a program in which young children are enrolled or in an agency which offers services to those who work with young children, the key to raising money is to *keep the request focused on the children.* That's obvious for child development centers, but no less important for professional development programs, membership associations, or other adult constituency organizations. These organizations simply need to describe their work in terms of how children will benefit, rather than how the money requested will help the organization, its students, or members.

Focusing the request on the children is more likely to create *an emotional connection* on the part of the donor, an important element in fundraising. An emotional connection is easiest to achieve in appeals to individuals, through the use of anecdotes or case examples. It's more difficult to accomplish in government grant applications, which require measurable outcomes linked to needs assessments, program design, evaluation processes, and proposed budgets. However, it's not impossible for these applications to evoke thoughts of little children with big needs.

The Fund Development Plan

"A goal without a plan is just a wish."
– Antoine de Saint Exupery

This book discusses a variety of fundraising strategies, but they will never be more than interesting ideas unless they fit inside a development plan that your organization has created — with specific objectives, action steps, assignments, and timelines.

The purpose of a fund development plan is to realize your organization's dreams of enough money to buy new equipment, remodel your space, launch a new professional development venture, hire additional staff, provide annual staff raises, serve more children, build a new facility, create a reserve fund, operate in the black each year, or any combination of these. Having a well thought out fund development plan is reassuring — it lets your board, staff, funders, and those you serve know that your organization will not have to operate in disaster mode if a major source of revenue falls away or a new regulation or program mandate creates unforeseen expenses.

Many fund development plans are created only after an organization has encountered a financial crisis. But fundraising in response to a crisis doesn't usually work — unless the crisis is something dramatic, like a fire that destroyed part of your facility, or a natural disaster that displaced your staff and clients. Cash flow problems or budget deficits won't help you raise money. Donors want to do something positive with their contributions — not cure an agency's financial woes.

The plan should be a joint creation of staff and board. Those who will implement it need to design it — not only to contribute their ideas, but also to build their excitement and enthusiasm.

Begin by identifying what you want to accomplish. How much money does the plan have to generate? For what purpose(s)? Over what time period? Try a three- to five-year plan, with *specific amounts* to be raised in each year. *Raising as much money as we can* is not precise enough to be motivating — how will you know when you've achieved that vague goal? Start with an amount that you believe to be doable — you'll want to experience success. Increase the goal in each succeeding year — again, by targeted amounts, either a specific dollar figure or a growth percentage. *Raising more money next year than this year* is not explicit enough — some might be satisfied with $2,500 more, while others might not feel the goal was truly achieved at less than $25,000.

The plan should address the following questions:

- From whom will you be requesting money? List the foundations, corporations, and civic groups you expect to ask along with the type of individuals you will be asking (see Chapter 2).

- How will you seek new funds — through grants? An annual letter-writing campaign? Special events? Memberships?

- When will you be asking for money? Foundation requests must be submitted according to the schedules established by each foundation. Some have specific deadlines, others accept proposals year-round. Deadlines for government grant applications are generally from four to six weeks after the availability of funding is announced. Although requests to individuals and corporations can be scheduled at almost any time, there are certain times that seem most appropriate for early childhood programs — these are discussed in Chapter 3.

- Who will be doing the asking? Do you have a board committee charged with fundraising? Will they need training or coaching? Who will do that and when will it occur?
- What materials will you need? Who will prepare them? When? Chapter 8 describes some of the materials that you'll want to develop.

The answers to each of these questions build the plan. Your plan should show every fundraising activity (special events, year-end appeal, newsletter inserts, foundation proposals, etc.), the target amount from each activity, the prospects for each (specific corporations, foundations, donor groups, etc.), a timeline for each activity, and who will be involved.

Who Holds the Key?

Fund development is seldom a favorite management activity in an early childhood program. Many people aren't comfortable asking others for money. Staff members are too busy; volunteers may not be willing to take it on. So it's often nobody's assigned job. In reality, it's *everyone's* job.

Specific individuals may be responsible for a particular fundraising activity, but everybody on your staff and on your board of directors has an important role to play in securing community support for your mutual work.

That role starts with everybody in the organization being ambassadors for the program. They have to be well informed: What does the program do?, Why is the program needed?, Why does it need additional money?, How will the money be used? — and they need to spread the word to their families, friends, neighbors, and business associates.

Spreading the word works well through informal contacts. When you meet someone for the first time who asks what kind of work you do, tell him or her not only what your job is, but also why it matters. You're not asking the person for money — at least not yet. But let that person know that your program depends on contributions from the community for support. If you are coping with funding cuts or unusually high costs, add that information. Encourage your staff to do the same with their new acquaintances. Fund development requires leadership by example. Those who *ask* for dollars must first *give* dollars. Individuals in top leadership roles (members of the board of directors, key staff) must give to the best of their ability before anyone else is asked. The amount doesn't matter, but the commitment does.

Some individuals resist this approach. They may feel that they give their all to the program for not enough pay (or, as a volunteer, *no* pay), and they resent being asked to dig into their own pockets to support it. But if they don't believe strongly, passionately about the good work the organization does, why should anyone else? How can they, in good conscience, ask others to support this important program if they, themselves, don't? And working for the program is not the same as supporting it, even if one feels that she or he is not paid in accordance with their true value. Working for wages below what one thinks is fair is not a form of in-kind donation.

Again, the amount of a contribution by a board or staff member is less important that the fact that the contribution is made. It's very powerful to be able to tell a potential donor "100% of our board and staff have contributed financially to our organization."

The Special Role of the Board

The boards of directors of early childhood programs are often populated by professionals in the field: directors of other programs, community college or university faculty, child life specialists, staff of related agencies, public school administrators, etc. While these individuals have much to offer in the way of programmatic knowledge, they are unlikely to be able to fulfill one of the most vital roles of non-profit boards — giving and getting money.

Few organizations are successful in raising funds from their communities without significant and sustained involvement by the board. Foundations and corporations tend to view board member involvement in fundraising as evidence of your agency's credibility and community support, while staff involvement may be seen as self-serving — after all, your salary depends on the fiscal health of the organization.

Further, 'well-connected' board members in the business and civic community can open doors for you. They have personal and professional relationships with people who can make or influence large contributions. While foundations or corporations are not likely to give you money merely because they are asked by someone they know, neither are they likely to refuse to meet with someone on your board with whom they are personally acquainted. Individual donors often make contributions when they are asked by a friend, family member, or colleague whose opinions they respect.

If your current board of directors does not have the capacity to raise the level of funds targeted in your fund development plan, then part of the plan has to include bringing in new people who have that ability. Start by adding them to current board membership and continue building your fundraising strength by filling future vacancies with these types.

How do you find and engage new people? Start by canvassing current board members to see what names they suggest. Ask who knows these individuals or who knows someone who knows them. Your local United Way might share its roster of key volunteers. These individuals may not agree to serve on your board, but they could refer you to other community-minded individuals. Your board chair should contact prominent law firms, banks, and area corporations, asking them to nominate employees to serve on your board. You won't enlist CEOs, but you could attract the community relations director or an associate who is on a rising career path. Welcome them — they will connect you to their peers, clients, and colleagues. Moreover, once you begin to recruit individuals who can 'give or get,' others will follow.

Your board chair should communicate to all board members, current and new, that each is expected to make a *personally significant contribution* each year. The amount will vary with each individual according to his or her financial status, but whatever the amount, it signifies the board member's commitment to the organization and willingness to accept responsibility for helping insure it has adequate resources.

CHAPTER 2

Whom Can We Ask (and Keep Asking) for Money?

One often hears the cliché, "It's not what you know, it's who you know." In fundraising, it's really, "Who knows you?"

Fundraising is guided by three basic ideas: 1) build a wide base of donors, 2) develop relationships with these donors, and 3) offer donors a variety of ways to support your organization.

Building the Donor Base

Fundraising starts with those who are closest to the organization — those who know it best — and moves outward from there. Visualize five concentric circles — each circle representing a relationship with your program:

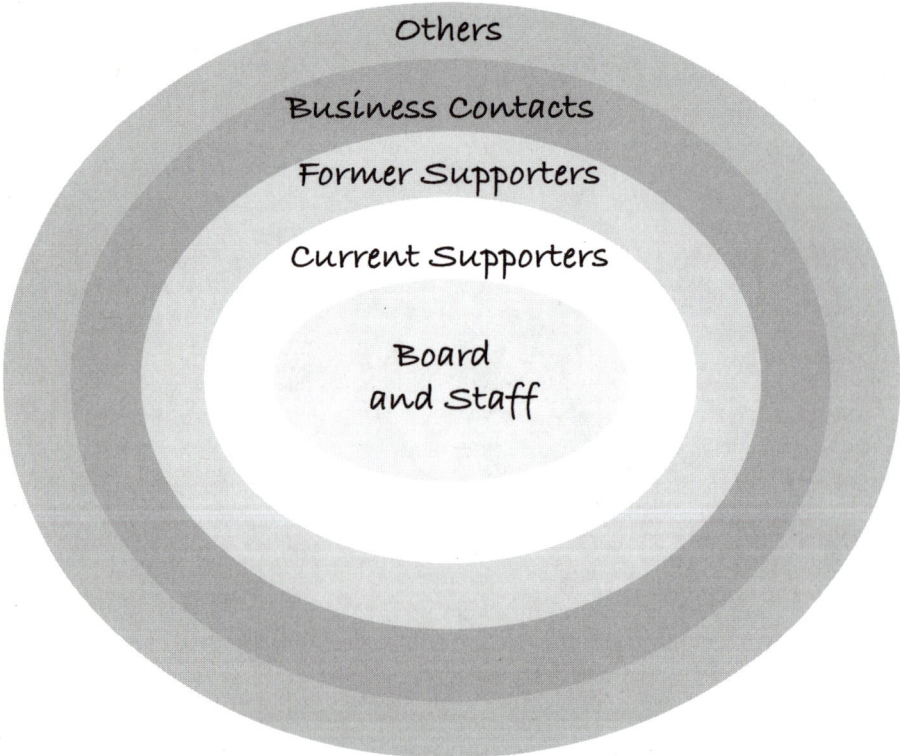

Adapted from Henry A. Russo, *Achieving Excellence in Fund Raising*, 1991.

The smallest, innermost circle represents your program's board and staff — the people at the organization's core. The next circle is made up of people *who already support your organization* — not only current contributors but, depending on the nature of your work, parents, members, students, or anybody else who uses your services, as well as your volunteers. You may not consider parents, members, students, or volunteers to be supporters, but think again. They know what your organization does and why, and they value it or they wouldn't be spending their money or time on it. They are already supporting the organization in one way — by paying for its services or contributing time. Offering them the opportunity to become donors allows them to support it more fully.

The question may arise as to whether participants in programs serving low-income populations should be asked to make contributions. Unless specifically prohibited by third-party funders' policies, all participants should be informed about the program's fundraising goals and invited to contribute as they are able. If they can't contribute themselves, they may be willing to ask their relatives, church members, employers, etc., to help.

The third circle consists of *former supporters* — people who have contributed in the past, as well as parents of children who have moved on from the program, former staff, former volunteers, etc. Much as private schools and colleges solicit contributions from graduates and their families, your organization should connect with its alumni.

Moving outward, the fourth circle includes *others with whom your organization has business and professional relationships.* There are a variety of prospects within this circle. Think about your vendors — the companies from whom you buy goods and services — educational supplies distributors, curriculum publishers, office supply stores, food wholesalers, supermarkets, your local bank, etc.

This circle might include groups such as the League of Women Voters, the Chamber of Commerce, and others who know you because you have ties to them through your board of directors, or because you've made presentations to them about the importance of the early childhood years.

This circle should also include early childhood professionals in your community — college faculty, consultants, directors of allied programs serving young children — as well as pediatricians and other clinicians who understand the importance of early childhood programs.

The fifth and largest circle includes *everyone else who might be interested in supporting your organization*, because they know and respect it or they simply care about young children. This would include friends, family, and neighbors of staff, board, and the parents/students/members you serve, foundations and corporations, and people who donate to other organizations serving young children and their families.

How do you find out who donates to programs for young children? Most agencies will not directly share their donor lists, but that doesn't mean you can't find out who supports them. One approach is to identify organizations in your community that actively raise money — you read about their fundraising events in your local paper or you've been asked to make a contribution, or you've heard (or seen, if new construction is underway) that they are expanding their services. Which organizations?

- children's hospital

- shelter for homeless families

- children's museum

- agency working with abused or neglected children

- local Boys and Girls Club

- YMCA/YWCA

- local chapter of the Make-A-Wish Foundation

- agencies serving children with special needs

- organizations serving specific populations similar to those you work with (children from low-income families, children who don't speak English, etc.)

Get on the mailing lists of some of these agencies — those that are closest in mission to your organization and those whose fundraising efforts are highly visible. Do so either by asking to be added or by making your own contribution. If the organization publishes a newsletter or annual report which acknowledges contributions by individual donors, you'll have your list of names. You'll need addresses, and finding them may be quite time-consuming. If possible, hire someone (a high school student) or try to find a volunteer to work on it. It's worth doing because the list is a pot of gold — names of people who have demonstrated their willingness and ability to give money to help young children in your community.

Some agencies may list their donors on their web sites — sometimes all of the contributors; more often, just the larger contributors, such as corporations, civic groups, and foundations. Again, that list is direct evidence of who has given money to causes similar to yours. And even if these agencies don't name their donors, their web sites often list their board membership. If that list includes board members' affiliations, it will give you information as to which businesses in your community are contributing time (and, probably, money) to the organization.

Developing Relationships with Your Donors

The concentric circles depict your organization's universe of donors — the people you will ask to contribute. Another construct, the fundraising pyramid, will help you think about how to increase their levels of support over time.

You begin your fundraising efforts by building a broad base of prospects who make small gifts. They give the least money and are the least committed to your organization, but these contributions are the easiest to get in terms of time and effort. By asking these donors to contribute more frequently (for example, a monthly contribution of $20), these small gifts will add up.

Your goal is to move as many donors as possible as far up the pyramid as possible, step-by-step. The number of donors decreases as you scale upward,

**Inspired
Donors**
Planned gifts

Invested Donors
Major gifts: large sums

Involved Donors
Established givers: frequent gifts, larger amounts

Informed Donors
Repeat givers: small but regular gifts

Identified Prospects
First-time givers: small gifts

Adapted from Michael J. Worth (ed). (2002). "Elements of the Development Program."
New Strategies for Educational Fund Raising.

but they will be more committed to your organization, and their
contribution amounts will be greater.

How do you move donors from the base to higher levels of the pyramid?
By building relationships with them.

Some people will make a small donation to test what you will do with it
and how you will respond to them. Large non-profits typically have
formulas which dictate their responses. For a small gift (however the
organization defines it), the donor gets a form letter, not individually
addressed. At a higher amount, a personalized letter is sent, signed by the

director of development. For a major gift, the letter is signed by the head of the organization or the chair of the board.

Your best bet, given that you will have a manageable pool of donors, is to acknowledge *every* donation in a personal manner. Handwritten notes are preferable — they don't have to be long, just sincere. For a large gift, a phone call followed by a handwritten note is a good idea, especially because a call is a more immediate response than a note or letter that has to work its way through the mail. A nice touch is to give the donor of a large gift a child's painting, attractively (but inexpensively) framed.

Interested donors will move up the pyramid when you regularly *inform* them about your program. Let people know how you will use their contributions, but don't stop there. Keep them apprised of the organization's activities through your newsletter, e-mail announcements of new funding or special recognition you've received, invitations to your annual meeting, or your *Week of the Young Child* celebrations.

Involve the donors you hope to move up the pyramid. Invite them to visit, to attend a meeting or conference with you, or send them articles that you come across that you think would be of interest. *Invest* them in your work by offering contributors naming opportunities. Such opportunities don't have to be limited to physical facilities — they can include program services, events, publications. If the commercial world can put names on football stadiums and the year-end games played in them, golf tournaments and lecture series, among other opportunities, the early childhood profession can find similar ways to recognize its most committed donors.

The top level of the pyramid is populated by the donors you have been able to *inspire*. This level will have the fewest individuals, will be the hardest to attain, and will likely take years of relationship-building or *cultivation*. But inspired donors will raise money for you and assign a substantial share of their assets to your organization through endowments, planned gifts, or bequests. These are the people who share your vision . . . who want to change children's lives in a measurable way and have the means to do so. Treasure them.

CHAPTER 3

Reaching Out, Taking In

The diagrams in the previous chapter depict how fundraising *relationships* develop according to 1) *proximity* (the concentric circles), and 2) *level of commitment* (the pyramid). Fundraising *approaches* should be implemented according to *effectiveness*, from those that bring you closest to the prospect (the most effective) to those where there is no personal contact at all (the least effective). This chapter focuses on the top five rungs of the 'Ladder of Effectiveness.'

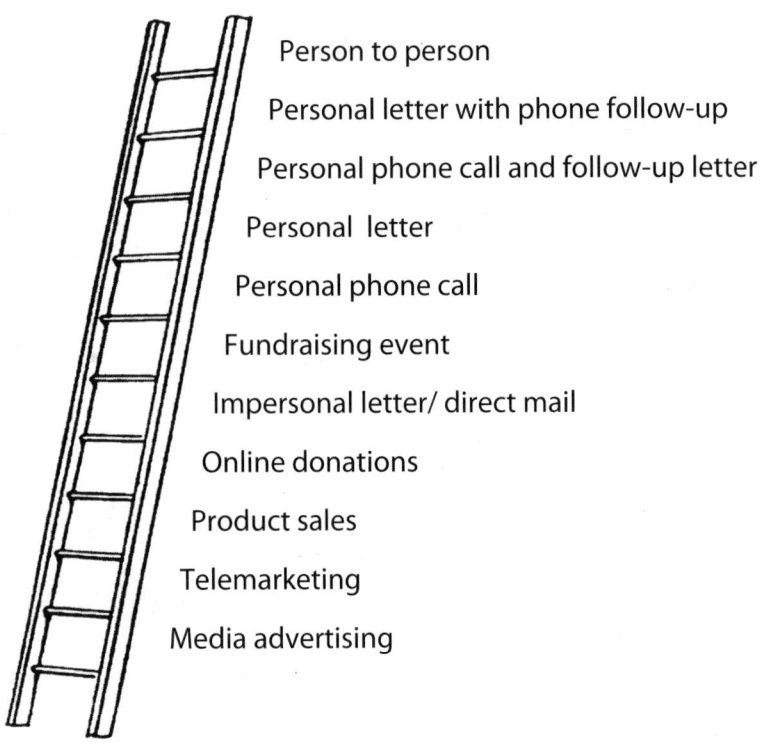

Person to person

Personal letter with phone follow-up

Personal phone call and follow-up letter

Personal letter

Personal phone call

Fundraising event

Impersonal letter/ direct mail

Online donations

Product sales

Telemarketing

Media advertising

Adapted from *The Ladder of Effectiveness*, The Fund Raising School, Center on Philanthropy, Indiana University, 2002.

Whether you believe the old fundraising adage, "people give to people," or embrace the philosophy that people give to visionary programs that inspire them, there is one inarguable principle: they don't give if they're not asked.

And though this book covers a number of ways of asking, person-to-person conversations with a prospect offer the best opportunity to create a personal connection between the prospect and your organization — to share your passion for the work and offer the other person the chance to help you in making a true and lasting difference in the lives of young children. You can make a request by letter, you can try it by phone, you can ask for help via your web site. But for a major gift (however you define it), there is no request as powerful as one that is delivered person-to-person.

Personal Visits

It is highly advisable to have the chairperson of your board make the request when you ask for a significant sum of money. Why? The board chair is seen as representing the community — a volunteer who has made his or her own personal commitment of time to the organization and, of course, a financial contribution. If you are calling upon a corporate executive, you might also bring a board member who works for or is close to someone who works for that company or a board member who is a corporate executive herself. If you are calling on a banker, a board member who does business with the bank would be a good choice. If you have a board member who is a personal friend of the prospect, so much the better.

The board chair presents a little information about the organization — whom it serves, how many are served, how long it's been in business — and what the need is. Have all of this information bulleted on one page that you can hand the prospect to review. Leave a folder with other information — your case statement, perhaps an architect's rendering if you are raising money for a new building (see Chapter 8), a list of board members, a summary of your program's accomplishments, and your latest newsletter.

As the program professional, you can answer any questions the prospect may have. It's helpful to anticipate objections. *It looks like the cost of caring for a baby in your program is nearly as much as college tuition — why?* Have good answers that will convince the prospect of the value of your program. How many low-income parents are you enabling to join the workforce? How well do your 'graduates' do when they arrive in kindergarten?

How many teachers have you trained and why is training so important? What does research say about children's early learning? How much is your program contributing to the local economy in payroll and operating costs?

Once the prospect has a feel for your organization, and before you have used up your allotted time (probably 30 minutes), the board chair should ask for the contribution. *Ed, can you/your company help the preschool with a contribution of $25,000?*

Ed may say, *I'll have to think it over.* Your board member should then reply, *We understand. When would be a good time for me to get back in touch with you?* Whatever Ed's response, you should make sure the board chair follows up at exactly that time.

Ed may say, *I need more information.* You should then reply, *I'd be happy to provide it. What information would be helpful? Would you like to schedule a visit to our preschool — maybe come for breakfast one day next week?* Follow up by getting the requested information to Ed as quickly as possible — dropping it off in person if necessary. If Ed will be visiting your program, make sure he sees it at its best and that your staff is prepared to answer questions or direct him to the person(s) who can answer.

Ed may say, *I/We can't make a $25,000 contribution, but I/we can probably manage $5,000.* Both you and your board chair should thank Ed sincerely now, and when the check is received. Don't let disappointment at the amount spoil the moment. You have a commitment for $5,000 more than you had when you walked in the door — and there's always the chance that you can come back for more in the future.

Ed may say, *We've committed all of our corporate contributions for this year, but we would be happy to consider a gift next year.* Thank him and ask how to make that request — do you need to send a letter? By what date? To whom? Follow Ed's instructions exactly.

Or, Ed may say, *I'm sorry. I/we won't be able to help you.* You and your board chair have no choice but to thank him graciously for his time, leave, and follow up with a brief note, again thanking him for his time. You can't ask Ed why he has refused to make a gift, but you can replay the visit. Was your presentation clear and to the point? What were his objections? Was there something you should have known (the company is having a bad year) or couldn't have known (the company announces the day after your visit that it is planning to relocate out of your community and Ed had agreed to the visit simply as a courtesy to your board chair). Even if you can't figure out why the request was turned down, don't burn your bridges. Ed may land at a different company in the future with more resources or more interest in young children.

Letters and Phone Calls

The other forms of personal contact (letters and phone calls) use similar strategies. Send a letter to the prospects, asking for a contribution and saying that (name of person) will be calling in a week to follow up. Board members who know the prospects should be asked to sign the letters and make the calls. If no board member is well acquainted with a prospect, your board chair signs the letter and makes the call. Include your packet of information with the letter, so the prospect will have had a chance to review it before the call. Some prospects, of course, will not have looked at your material when the call is made, but those who have may have questions. If the board member is unable to answer any question, be sure you follow up quickly.

When your board member has left two or more messages for the prospect over a period of two to three weeks and received no response, the next conversation should be with the prospect's assistant or someone else in the company that the board member might know. The idea is to find out when the best time would be to try to catch the prospect on the phone. If that's not possible, your board member can try e-mailing the prospect and asking directly for a time to call. It's not difficult to uncover someone's business e-mail address . . . look at the company's web site, which may list staff contacts, or click on the 'contact us' form to see what the e-mail address format is.

These suggestions underscore the importance of having board members who already have personal relationships with your organization's key prospects — they are much more likely to get a response. Since it is often harder to get an appointment to see or speak with an influential person than it is to get the gift you are requesting, don't be disappointed if you can't get in front of him or her. Just keep looking for that person who can open the door for you.

CHAPTER 4

Inviting, Writing, and Spotlighting

This chapter covers the middle three rungs of the 'Ladder of Effectiveness' — fundraising events, direct mail, and online donations.

Events — Yours and Theirs

Events require staff and volunteer time and effort, whether you're planning a pancake breakfast, a black-tie gala, or a golf tournament. Big events call for sponsorships or underwriting — contributions to cover the event's expenses, so that the funds raised can all be dedicated to the organization. Since at least some of these expenses must be paid well in advance (rental of facilities, professional fees, advertising, etc.), the event's proceeds (and, in the worst-case scenario, the agency's budget) are at risk unless sufficient underwriting is secured.

The major advantage of events over other forms of fundraising is the opportunity to increase your program's visibility, especially if it is a 'signature event' — a one-of-a-kind occasion to which your name is attached, year after year. All of the publicity will feature your name and, in many cases, something about your work. Further, some people who know little or nothing about your agency will participate in the event, not because it benefits your organization, but because they are interested in the event itself: they play golf or they enjoy 5K runs, they've been invited to 'fill a table' at a luncheon or dinner, or they want to hear the speaker who will be appearing. Once they attend, you have the chance to 'hook' them . . . to inform them (in an interesting way) about your services and to make sure they enjoy the event, so they'll come back next time.

For many organizations, the ideal event is one sponsored by some other group who assumes the financial risk and whose members are experienced at conducting events. As the beneficiary, your agency may be asked to help in some way — sending board members on the sponsor's visits to underwriting prospects, making some of the arrangements, submitting invitation lists, or providing volunteers to help at the event itself, but the major responsibilities lie with the sponsor.

The sponsoring groups are likely to be among the most visible in your community (a Rotary Club, the Junior League, etc.), so they should be easy to find. Some will pick an agency to be their beneficiary for an extended period of time; others will change the beneficiary(ies) each year. Being the recipient of funds every year gives you a predictable source of support for operating expenses, a scholarship fund, or other recurring need. Funds available to you in just one year can be targeted toward a special program, project, or capital need. Whether you are seeking $50,000 each year from an annual tennis tournament or a one-time sum of $500,000 from a charity ball to help build your new facility, your challenge is not only to convince the sponsoring group to select your organization as its beneficiary, but also to encourage its members to feel that they've made the best possible choice. If you meet this challenge, the members may become individual donors to your program, even after the group has moved on to another beneficiary.

You don't need to limit your sights to civic or social groups. New specialty stores, restaurants, and the like often plan 'openings' to which they invite the movers and shakers in your community and which usually feature a pre-selected beneficiary. Similarly, the opening night of the circus or other commercial entertainment venue may be staged as a benefit. Don't bother with arts organizations, such as the opera, symphony, or ballet — their opening night benefits are understandably planned to raise funds for their own work.

Openings are most often staged by public relations firms, so think about getting to know some firms in your area and, even better, inviting the head of one of them onto your board.

The retail industry also may be a source of event fundraising. In at least three large cities, well-known retailers (clothing stores, bookstores, gift shops, jewelers, sporting goods distributors, among others) offer 20% discounts for a nine-day period in late October/early November to people who have purchased a special card benefiting a local non-profit. The card currently sells for $60; proceeds from the card sales go directly to the agency. The agency's volunteers sign up additional retailers each year.

In this model, only the agency in each city who created this event benefits, but a national department store chain has adopted a similar plan — non-profits are invited to sell discount cards good for one designated day of shopping. The non-profit keeps all of the proceeds of the card sales (currently $10) and receives an additional sum (currently $3) for every pre-sold card redeemed at the store. While the store can point with pride to the total amount generated for the non-profit community, the modest price of the card suggests that a great many will have to be sold by any single agency in order to realize a significant amount of money.

Direct Mail

There is probably not a single household in your community that doesn't receive as much unwanted mail as the mailbox will hold. Among this clutter are various fundraising appeal letters from charitable organizations — some better known than others. These letters are easily recognized — with their non-profit rate, bulk-mail postage, and their mailing labels or high-volume imprint envelopes. Many of them go directly into the trash, without ever being opened.

Because the response rate is usually quite low (0.5% to 2%), the mailing lists for these appeals number in the hundreds of thousands or more. These are names of *potential* prospects — individuals who have given to other charities, who subscribe to certain publications, who live in targeted ZIP codes, or who comprise a defined demographic. The appeal letter is carefully crafted and test-marketed before being mailed. Premiums (address labels, note pads, etc.) may be included. The letter is commercially printed; a direct mailing house handles the actual mailing.

This approach is expensive and inefficient for most early childhood organizations. However, you can be successful with much smaller and more targeted direct mail efforts using the prospects who have been identified within the concentric circles. Assuming this list numbers in the hundreds, rather than thousands, send a personalized letter to each (*Dear Mr. Green* rather than *Dear Friend*). Plan to use first-class postage — the letter is more likely to be opened.

If possible, send a letter two to four times per year since donors frequently don't give the first time they are asked, but may well contribute after additional reminders. Moreover, many donors who give once in a year will give again.

At the very least, plan a year-end appeal. Most non-profits send out requests toward the end of the calendar year to take advantage of the spirit of giving that takes hold as the holidays approach and because donors typically make tax-deductible contributions at that time as part of their year-end tax planning. *donate to a project or cause instead of gifts, etc.*

In order to avoid your letter being lost in the December shuffle, have it written and your prospect list (names and current addresses) ready by October 1. You won't send the letter until early or mid-November (dated as of that time), but you want to have everything prepared.

The letter should be signed by your board chair. Distribute the mailing list to all of your board members, so they can identify people they know. Ask them to write a brief note at the bottom of the page on the letters going to those individuals. This takes some organizing — you'll need to get the completed letters to the board members in sufficient time to add their notes before your mailing deadline. It's easiest if you can separate the letters by board member and distribute them at a board meeting. Otherwise, in the case of board members who miss the meeting, you have to arrange a time with each individual board member to write his/her notes. It's definitely worth the effort — there's nothing more effective than a personal, hand-written note on a fundraising letter, which says something like, *I really believe in The Parent Resource Center's work. I hope you can help.*

great idea

A good time to schedule a direct mail appeal to those who did not respond to the year-end appeal is in February, around Valentine's Day. Valentines made by children, featuring children, or requests tied to 'issues of the heart' can be very effective. It's probably too soon to send an appeal to anyone who made a year-end donation, but you can certainly send them a Valentine. Some tried and true ideas:

- *Heartfelt thanks!* on a felt, cut-out heart

- *Your Heart's in the Right Place* on card stock decorated by the children

- a heart sticker affixed to your agency's informal stationery notes with a hand-written message (*thanks for being a friend* or *we love you*)

- a black and white photo of children with small red or pink heart stickers placed appropriately on each print, with an appropriate message enclosed.

Since writing messages by hand or putting stickers on stationery or photos is time-consuming, make it a team effort.

If your organization features a special summer program or something similar that is date-specific, send out an appeal about six to eight weeks ahead of that time, featuring whatever it is you are planning, and explaining why it is so important and needs the prospect's support.

If you don't have a date-specific program, try an appeal tied to a back-to-school theme, for mailing no later than the end of August. Focus on how your program helps prepare children for school or on the fact that little children are learning from birth.

You'll notice that the appeal letters that you receive from large, national non-profits are usually four pages of text — either one sheet folded in half and printed front to back on each side of the fold or two sheets of paper, printed on each side. They're always written in short, punchy paragraphs.

The idea is that if the organization can interest the reader — get the reader to go through the whole letter so he'll have a fuller understanding of the organization and the need it meets, the more likely he'll make a contribution.

Four-page letters with short paragraphs are hard to write. The non-profits that do so have direct mail departments full of writers or they contract with direct mail consultants. If you don't have access to those resources, aim for a well-written, one-page letter, also with short paragraphs, that states your request simply and directly. Start with a declarative statement.

- *ABC Preschool needs your help.* Tell how the person can help.

- *They called it Head Start* for a reason. Explain why.

- *It's been said that good things come in small packages.* Write about your services for the smallest children in the community (the youngest), your work with children in small groups, the small size of your center, or whatever about your organization might lend itself to this statement.

- *It costs us $x,000 a year to keep our classrooms supplied with red paint.* Use that in conjunction with a Valentine appeal or change to *red, white, and blue paint* in conjunction with a July appeal, or refer to the colors used in a child's artwork featured on your brochure.

Follow the opening statement with an explanation of what your agency is, what it does, and why you are asking for money. What are the funds for? What difference will this donation make to your program? To the life of a child?

End your letter by asking for the gift:

 You can help make this happen with a contribution of . . .

 Please give generously and know that your gift will help give 50 children a better start in life.

It's worthwhile developing a specific letter for each of the prospect groups comprising the concentric circles described in Chapter 2. Like any effort to persuade, you need diverse messages for diverse audiences. The auto industry doesn't use the same advertising images or written copy to sell sports cars as they do to sell mini-vans. The prospects for these products are different, so the messages are different as well.

For individuals who are closest to you — who know the organization and its work — you don't have much to explain.

Focus the letter on why their help is needed. The further out the circles go, the more you'll need to explain what the organization is and why the work is so important.

In addition to appeal letters, your newsletter can be a fundraising tool. Every issue you publish should have a list of the most recent donors (names, not amounts). The newsletter should also include a pre-printed remittance/reply envelope — typically 6.5" wide by 3.25" high — that might look something like this:

Inside of Flap

---

gummed area

I want to help. Enclosed is my tax-deductible gift of:
❏ $500   ❏ $250   ❏ $100   ❏ $50   ❏ other_____

❏ I am enclosing my check payable to Country Hill Child Development Center
❏ I am making my donation by credit card
❏ Visa   ❏ MasterCard   ❏ AMEX   ❏ Discover

Card Number _____ Exp. Date_____

Name_____

Address_____

City/State/ZIP_____

Phone_____ E-mail_____

Back of envelope

This gift is made:

In Honor of _____

In Memory of_____

Name_____

Address_____

City, State, ZIP_____

Or, the back of the envelope may list the items that donations at varying levels will support or the various 'funds' that your organization has established:

Here's how you can help:

Your gift of **$25** will purchase diapers for one infant for one week

Your gift of **$50** will provide snacks for five children for one month

Your gift of **$100** will buy new books for one classroom

Your gift of **$250** will support one week of care for a six-month-old child

Your gift of **$500** will enable us to help 25 parents find child care

Thank You for caring!
Country Hill Child Development Center

I would like my gift used as follows:

- ❏ scholarship fund
- ❏ building fund
- ❏ parent education program
- ❏ summer day camp
- ❏ Fund for The Future (endowment)
- ❏ general fund

Make sure that your newsletter goes not only to your 'regular' mailing list, but also to all donors and prospects. Why? The donors will see that you are publicly thanking them for their gift, in addition to the personal thank-yous you send. The prospects will see that other people give to your organization. And both groups will better understand your organization by reading about its work.

Online Donations

There should be an easy way for visitors to find your web site, and once there, an easy way to make online contributions. Try to have a web address that someone could guess if they don't already know it: www.HappyHillPreschool.org is better than www.EarlyLearning.org, even though 'early learning' is what your preschool is all about. Think of your web address as a listing in the white pages — what people will look up — as opposed to a display ad in the yellow pages — what they will want to know about your program. The actual site will tell them that when they get there.

If you want to make sure your web site can be easily found, ask several people (friends, neighbors, etc.), who don't know your web address, to try to find it and let you know how many attempts it took. If they haven't found it within two or three tries, consider changing your web address.

44

People frequently use search engines to find particular web sites. They'll get to you if you have used the appropriate keywords that will enable search engines to home in on your web site. Among the keywords you MUST have are your organization's name and city and relevant terms about the service(s) you provide. However, if the terms are too general (*infants, young children, early childhood, parents, training*), your listing will disappear far down the ranking of programs that also use these words. Moreover, you may generate visits by individuals who are looking for products and services that you don't offer (nursery furniture, adoption, pediatrics, fitness classes, etc.).

Brainstorm with your staff and/or board keywords that are unique to your program. Then use these words on each page of your web site, making sure they appear toward the top of the page, are prominently displayed in headings, and are repeated often (without boring the reader). Each time you add a new page to your web site or even post a new feature, be sure to incorporate your keywords.

Your web site address should be shown on all of your print materials. Include it in a postscript to every fundraising letter you send informing the readers that they can make online contributions if they wish.

Your web site is your showcase — a place to spotlight your program with photos and text and graphics depicting how valuable your work is. Keep the information simple and focused. Every page should strive for that desired emotional connection with the prospect, and every page should have a link (*Donate Now*) that takes the visitor directly to the page on which the person can make his or her gift.

Every page should also have your mailing address and your telephone number, as subtle validation that you really do exist to provide the services you have described so eloquently.

Web sites offer an especially effective method of encouraging donors to make frequent contributions by enabling them to pledge monthly amounts by credit card. A $30-per-month gift ("only $1 dollar per day") seems more affordable than a year-end $360 gift. Focus on obtaining these monthly gifts . . . and on showing appreciation for them. Knowing in advance that your program will receive regular donations not only gives you and your board additional peace of mind, it also shows potential funders that you have a diverse and predictable revenue stream.

Your agency does not have to collect online donations itself. There are several companies who, for a fee, will manage a secure gift-giving process on your web site that results in the prompt deposit of donors' credit card charges into your agency's bank account, generates a pre-written thank-you letter (although, for a manageable number of donors, a more personalized letter is preferable), and allows you to track and analyze contributions. Talk with other non-profits in your community to find out who manages their credit card donations and ask how satisfied they are. In addition to the cost of the service, evaluate the technical assistance that is offered. If your organization is new to the online donation process, you'll value the availability of responsive technical support.

CHAPTER 5

Grant: Wasn't He Our 18th President?

What is a Grant?

A grant is an amount of money given in response to a proposal that describes some activity to be conducted in response to a need.

A grant differs from a donation (even though the amount may be the same), because a grant comes with defined expectations on the part of the grantor (foundation or civic group). You (the grantee) said you would do something specific with the money to benefit those you serve or would like to serve, and you have to do it and report on it.

A donor is usually motivated to give your group money by his or her own sense of charity, plus a favorable impression of your program. Donors, while demonstrating support, are unlikely to be interested in the details of how you do the work, who the key staff members are, and other aspects of the 'insides' of the organization.

A grantor, on the other hand, gives money to address a particular concern or area of interest — child development, early learning, women's issues, etc. Grantors will want to know your agency's approach to addressing its concerns, how capable you are of meeting the need you've identified, how you will spend the money, and how you (and they) will know if the money was well spent.

A grant is also different from a *contract*. A contract is usually much more specifically defined — it is an agreement between parties that stipulates exactly what your organization will do, how it will do it, and how much it will be paid to do it. A contract is solicited — your county government needs an agency to manage child care subsidies and puts out a request for proposal (RFP), request for quote (RFQ), or request for application (RFA), to which your agency responds as to *how you will do what the county wants done*.

Federal programs such as *Head Start, Early Head Start, Early Reading First*, as well as some state programs, are referred to as 'grant' funding, even

NOT JUST SMALL CHANGE

though they are solicited like a contract. The government agency publishes a funding announcement with specific components that must be addressed by the applicant. The difference is that for these opportunities, you propose *what you will do* in response to the components (**your** program design), while for the child care subsidy management request, you describe *how you will fulfill* the contract requirements (**their** program design).

Foundation grants offer the most opportunity for innovation and creative solutions, followed by government grants, while contracts are the most restrictive. They all require written proposals, and they are all solid sources of revenue.

Finding Funding Sources and Building Relationships with Them

Writing a proposal and sending it to every funding source you can think of is a waste of time and diminishes your credibility. Instead, search for the right sources. Go to the library and look at various foundation directories, or head right to the Internet. Many foundations, corporations, and government agencies include information on funding opportunities on their web sites. Other sites provide the information found in printed foundation directories (see Chapter 9).

If you are unsure of whose web sites to check, try this list:

- corporations headquartered in your city or state

- corporations headquartered elsewhere, but doing business in your city (large retailers, delivery companies, etc.)

- corporations that cater to the clients you serve (manufacturers of products for young children)

- federal agencies (Departments of: Health & Human Services; Housing and Urban Development; Education; Environmental Protection Agency; and so on)

- state health, human services, and education agencies

- local health, human services, education, and community development agencies

- foundations in your community

- foundations in your state

- national foundations

- organizations that are similar to yours; they often post information on their web sites about grants they've received, or they may list their major donors

When you are doing this kind of research, or *prospecting*, there is information you will want to gather, use, keep, and update. The form on the adjacent page is an example of the information to gather. Make copies of it and complete the form for each funding source you are considering, especially foundations.

If you are using a directory as your primary source of information, it's a good idea to call the funding source to confirm information as to the organization's current address and the name of the person to whom your proposal should be sent. Call, too, if you're not sure whether to apply or how much to apply for. Pre-proposal phone conversations or face-to-face meetings are an accepted (and expected) step in the proposal process with many foundations and corporations.

Note that the *Prospect Form* has a section called *Action Taken*. The last item — the date you sent the thank-you letter — is as important as the date you sent the proposal. Most people know to thank a funder when a grant is awarded. Not all of them know to thank the funder for considering their proposal if they didn't get the grant. That's critical. And not all of them know to ask for feedback.

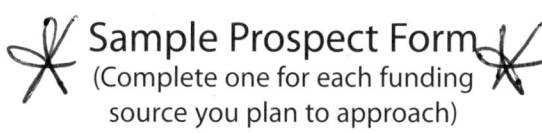

Sample Prospect Form
(Complete one for each funding source you plan to approach)

Contact Information
Name of funding source _____
Contact person _____
Address _____
Phone _____
Web address _____
Trustees _____

Is This a Good Match?
Interest areas (in order listed) _____
Geographical restrictions _____
Types of support (capital, operating, project) _____
Total grants paid for reporting period _____
Grantees, amounts _____
Dollar range of grants (smallest to largest) _____
Average grant amount
  (divide total grants paid by number of grants) _____
Typical grant amount
  (may differ from average if dollar range is very wide) _____

Application Information
Are there application guidelines or forms? _____
Initial approach (letter or proposal) _____
Deadlines _____
Trustees meeting dates _____

Action Taken
Proposal sent   Date _____
Proposal acknowledged   Date _____
Follow-up information requested   Date _____
Follow-up information sent   Date _____
Grant awarded/declined   Date _____
Thank-you letter sent   Date _____
  (whether or not grant awarded)

51

 When you *do* get the grant, in the process of thanking the funder, ask if the person would be willing to share with you what he saw as the proposal's strengths and whether there were any weaknesses. This information will help you as you prepare proposals to others in the future.

Your thank-you letter has to be written, but you can ask for the feedback by phone. In fact, it's a good idea to call the funder as soon as you receive the letter informing you of a grant award. At that time, you can tell him how thrilled your organization is and how good it feels to have the funder's support, and so on. That's a good time to ask for the feedback.

If you learn of your grant award in a phone call from the funder, plunge right ahead into thanking him and asking for the feedback. In either event, follow up with a written thank-you.

Contact with the funder does not end with your thank-you letter. Most funders will ask for reports at various intervals or at the end of your project. Send the report when it's due and, again, mention the importance of this grant to your work.

 Even if the funder doesn't request a report, it's a nice touch to send one. Also, send a note any time your agency receives funding from another source for the project. That validates the first funder's decision to support you.

If an article about your project appears in your local newspaper or in a professional newsletter, send a note along with a copy of the article.

 If you receive a letter from someone who benefits from your grant-funded project, send a copy to the funder. If you hold an event related to the project (ribbon-cutting, program launch, etc.), invite the funder (even if the foundation or corporation is far away). If he attends, introduce him to the other attendees, either as part of the program, or individually. If he cannot attend, send a copy of the printed program with a nice note.

If your project includes a product of any kind (a publication or video), send a copy of the product to the funder.

Keep the funder on your mailing list for newsletters, holiday wishes, and other contacts. Show them that they made a good choice in funding your agency.

But what if they don't fund you?

You can ask for feedback in your 'thank you for your consideration letter.' If you know the individual personally, you can call. What will you hear? Probably that your proposal was excellent, but they had many excellent proposals and couldn't fund them all. That is probably true and might make you feel better, but it's not at all helpful. While government agencies are obligated to give you feedback, foundations and corporations are not. So don't be surprised if they don't tell you anything, but ask anyway.

Also, don't be afraid to re-submit a proposal in the next funding cycle. If your program is a fit with what the source funds, it may take two or three tries before you are funded. Perhaps a different project related to your program will have more appeal. Or the fact that you've had another year of success or that you were funded by some other organizations since your first proposal submission will help.

Your Organization's Credibility

Your agency's credibility has as much (or more) influence on your chances of winning a grant as the project you are proposing. Your program must be credible in terms of what it does, whom it serves, and how it works; and it should have some solid accomplishments. All of this can be summarized in your *credibility file* — a collection of items that attest to how worthwhile your program is and how deserving it is of funding.

Your credibility file should include articles about the agency or articles about trends and events in which you are quoted; letters from parents or other agencies or public figures, or experts in your field; printed programs from conferences at which you've presented; statistics on the people you serve; positive comments from funding sources or licensing representatives or other community authorities; and requests from other organizations for your program's services, and the like.

Another source of credibility consists of newspaper, magazine, and journal articles on any of the relevant issues you deal with — the importance of the early years, infant development, literacy and language, the changing demographics of your community, and so on. When you use these articles, you are 'borrowing' the credibility of the source mentioned in the article, whether it's the census bureau presenting updated figures on child poverty in your city, a university researcher reporting a new study on children's learning, a noted expert testifying before the legislature, or anyone else who is supporting the need for which you are requesting funds.

Start clipping and saving these articles when you see them. You can't rely on a major news magazine printing an article on brain development when it comes time for you to write a proposal to fund an additional infant classroom. Just be careful that you don't use clippings that are more than a year or two old — 'stale' information will eventually diminish your credibility.

In addition, get together with your staff to brainstorm what you already have that attests to your credibility. Maybe it's the number of calls you get from the community inquiring about your services, the number of families on your waiting list, the number of volunteer hours dedicated to the program, thank-you notes from clients you've served or colleagues you've worked with, and so on. Think creatively and use whatever you've got. The form on the adjacent page can be used to summarize what you have available and what you need to gather.

Your written proposal should emphasize your credibility in every way. Be sure to send a cover letter or other correspondence on agency letterhead, with the names of your board of directors (and, if room, their affiliations) prominently displayed. The more recognizable the names (people, businesses) or titles (Judge, Doctor, Reverend, etc.), the better. However, don't list impressive names if they're not actually on your board of directors. Instead, work on adding such individuals to your board as openings occur.

Sample
Credibility File Summary

Item	Source	Date(s)*	Copy attached (√) or where filed
article(s) about agency			
article(s) in which staff are quoted			
letters from parents			
letters from other agencies			
letters from public figures			
letters from experts			
programs from conferences where staff presented			
number of inquiry calls			
number on waiting list			
client statistics			
number of volunteer hours			
comments from funding sources			
comments from licensing staff			
requests from other agencies for services			
subcontracts with other agencies			
articles on early childhood, brain development, etc. List: _____			
Others: _____			

*Out-of-date articles or letters lose their power. Don't use them after one year . . . two at the most.

Preparing to Prepare the Proposal

Your job in writing a proposal is to explain your request so clearly, compellingly, and convincingly that funders will give you money. What you write has to be well thought out and well written. It has to tell your story in a way that captures the reader's interest at the beginning and holds it throughout.

Proposal writing requires an orderly thought process: the ability to conceptualize, to proceed from an idea to a written plan, and the skill to describe the plan clearly, concisely, and appealingly. It requires a high level of attention to detail — not only with regard to what the proposal says, but also to what it doesn't say. The writer must be able to see the gaps — what questions might be raised in the mind of the reader? What loose ends have been left dangling? What is in the budget that hasn't been described in the proposal narrative, or what's in the narrative that isn't reflected in the budget?

If you don't have the time to take on the task, or you don't feel that you are the best person to do it, find someone else inside your organization or outside of it who can write proposals for you. You want to put your best foot forward with your first submission.

If you decide to contract with someone outside of the organization to write your proposals, you can conduct an Internet search for a grant writer, contact other non-profits in your community to seek referrals to grant writers with whom they have contracted or to ask if they have individuals on staff whom they would permit to moonlight for you on a non-competing basis, or locate the nearest chapter of the Association of Fundraising Professionals, which lists grant writers seeking work. Expect to pay anywhere from $50 to $100 per hour, depending on the experience of the grant writer and the going rate in your area. Some grant writers may agree to work for a flat fee based on the number of hours they estimate the project will take. Most reject the idea of working on a contingency basis: being paid a percentage of the monies received from their grant proposals. They prefer to be paid for their time, just as other professionals are. They understand that funders want the dollars they award to support the proposed work, not pay the cost of writing the proposal (government funding specifically prohibits such payment). Finally, there are many reasons why a well-written proposal may not be funded that have nothing to do with the grant writer's skill. It's unfair to penalize the grant writer, especially when the same proposal may be re-submitted and funded in the future, or used as the basis of a revised, ultimately successful proposal.

Whoever writes the proposal should not work in isolation. There should be a shared planning process with brainstorming about the proposed project, as well as the kind of data you'll need to support it. Bring together the staff within your organization who have expertise related to the proposed project, along with staff who may know very little about it. Why this latter group? Because they can challenge your assumptions and ask the hard questions. You'll want your own team to challenge the logic and appropriateness of what you propose, not the funder.

Only one person should actually write the proposal. Others can contribute information and ideas; some may draft sections of the proposal. But there is nothing worse than a proposal that reads like it was put together by a committee. People write in the same way they talk, with a particular rhythm, style, and use of language, and a proposal written by more than one person will reflect those differences. The goal is a proposal that is as smooth and as flowing as possible — one that engages the reader, so that he or she wants to keep on reading.

Once you have completed your first draft, give it back to the others. Ask them to check it for accuracy — have you captured all the data, are all expenses reflected in the budget, are job titles correct? Does the proposal make sense to them? Does it read well? Ask one or two people who have not been part of the proposal-writing process to read it as well — they're likely to point out areas where reviewers might have questions.

Ask Jen :

The Basics of Proposal Preparation

Every proposal you submit must follow these rules:

1. It must look neat and orderly. The look of your proposal gives the
    funding source a sense of how your organization approaches a task.
    No matter how worthy the project, if the proposal itself looks
    sloppy, is disorganized, or is hard to follow, it can be discarded
    without having been read.

2. There can be no spelling or typographical errors. Be sure the name
    of the person to whom you are sending the proposal is correctly
    spelled and that there are no typos anywhere in the proposal.
    Proofread it twice and then ask someone else to do so a third time.
    It's difficult to proofread something you've written yourself, because
    you tend to see what you think you've written, not what you've
    actually written. You're so familiar with what the proposal *should*
    say that you may not see what it *does* say. And don't rely on your
    word processing software to check your spelling — you may have
    typed a word that is correctly spelled, but is not the word you
    intended to use. Use the proofreader's form on the adjacent page;
    if you use several proofreaders, ask each to use a copy of the form.

3. There can be no calculation errors. Check and re-check the
    proposal budget and any other calculations you may have shown.
    For example, if you cite the number of children you serve according
    to age percentages (18% infants, 25% toddlers, 34% three-year-olds,
    etc.), the percentages must add up to 100%. If you calculate a cost
    per unit of service, be sure that you have correctly multiplied the
    number of units per client by the number of clients and that you
    have accurately divided that total into your cost.

4. It must follow the funding source's format. If a foundation wants a
    two-page letter, don't send three pages. If they want a proposal
    section called *Statement of the Problem*, don't call it *Needs*

Sample Proofreader Review

Name_____

Date proposal read_____

Check carefully for the following:

- ❑ proposal follows funder's format (number of pages, sequence of narrative, etc.)

- ❑ language reflects that of funder (e.g., statement of **problem** or statement of **need**, proposed **program** or **project**, etc.)

- ❑ all requirements stipulated by funder (e.g., grant evaluation criteria) are addressed

- ❑ correct spelling of names; correct titles

- ❑ correct spelling of words

- ❑ no typographical errors

- ❑ no grammatical errors

- ❑ correct punctuation

- ❑ page numbers are in sequence

- ❑ page numbers agree with table of contents

- ❑ page numbers agree with cross references in text (e.g., *see page 12*)

- ❑ no calculation errors in the budget

- ❑ budget numbers agree with budget narrative

- ❑ appendices or attachments appear in the sequence in which they are referred to in the text

- ❑ all requested attachments are included (audit, IRS determination letter, Board of Directors list, etc.).

I have read the attached proposal and made corrections and/or identified items needing correction or clarification.

Signature _____

Statement, even if you've called it that in every other proposal you've ever submitted. Mirror the funding source's language throughout the proposal. Similarly, follow the assembly instructions. Put everything in the order requested by the funder. Use binder clips, paper clips, rubber bands, or whatever else is stipulated. Even though you may be asked to send more than one copy of the proposal, assume that at least some of the pages you are submitting will be photocopied, so unless stapling is specifically requested, leave the document unstapled.

5. It must be tailored to the individual funding source. This means creating different proposals for the same project, depending upon what each funding source is interested in. What will be different in each proposal is the focus . . . and you'll know what to focus on from the information you gathered in your research on funding sources. For example, a child care agency serving low-income families could focus on the importance of its pre-literacy activities for a foundation that is interested in early education. It could highlight its services to the working poor for a foundation that targets its funding toward alleviating poverty. Its proposal could focus on how its program benefits women and girls for a foundation interested in these types of programs.

CHAPTER 6

Writing Foundation Proposals: Dear Mr. Gates

The good news about foundations is that there are literally thousands of them, with hundreds of billions of dollars in assets. Some are small, family foundations whose grants are narrowly defined or whose gifts are restricted to pre-determined organizations. Some are large, community-based foundations that administer donor-advised funds, with grants made to agencies in the area in which the foundation is located. Others are huge, nationally-recognized funders that make grants of significant size throughout the world. And there is every size in between.

The not-so-good news is that, just as you see them as a potential source of funding, so does nearly every other non-profit. Your foundation proposal could be one of hundreds in the stack to be reviewed — if it hasn't been screened out initially. Further, there is often a long lead-time between submission of your proposal and a decision. Some foundations' boards meet only once or twice a year. Even those that meet quarterly, monthly, or 'as needed' may not act on your proposal soon enough for their funding to meet your timeframe. They may defer action until they learn more about your organization, they may have distributed all of their annually available funds before your proposal arrived, or they may decide to review only some of the requests in that towering stack. Finally, many foundations are more interested in underwriting specific projects than contributing to operating expenses. Since many early childhood organizations' primary funding needs relate to day-to-day operations, seeking funding from foundations may not be the answer.

So why not end this chapter here?

Countless early childhood programs have had remarkable success with foundations, including one that asked a foundation for $150,000 and received $200,000.

Success with foundation funding begins with research: which foundations have set funding priorities that match your agency's work? Which foundations have given to agencies similar to yours? Which foundations are located in your community or state? Which foundations have given to organizations in your community or state? Use the resources in Chapter 10 to help you with your research.

The answers to the questions from the previous paragraph create a list of potential funders. The list must then be whittled down. If you are seeking funds for a building project, eliminate any foundations that say they don't contribute to capital campaigns. If yours is a faith-based program, cross off any foundations that give only to secular groups. If you are seeking a grant of $100,000, don't bother with foundations whose largest grants are in the $2,000-$3,000 range. Since numerous foundations don't fund requests for operating support, think about whether you can package aspects of your operating budget into time-limited 'projects' (staff training, a classroom literacy initiative, parent programs, etc.). If your operating needs don't lend themselves to the project approach, don't apply to these foundations.

One of the most effective ways of determining whether a foundation would be a good fit with your organization is to make a preliminary contact. You can call the foundation or write a letter of inquiry. In fact, many foundations require a letter of inquiry or intent before an applicant submits a proposal. Because foundations can use these letters to screen out potential applicants, it is critical that your letter have a brief, well-written description of the need, how you plan to address it, and the amount requested. Like the proposal summary discussed later in this chapter, it should preview the proposal itself — you don't want to make up the letter of inquiry as you go along and later find that what you wrote doesn't agree with the actual proposal. The contact is preliminary, but the proposal should already be close to final.

Whether you make the initial contact by phone or by letter, briefly introduce your agency and what you are seeking funds for, state your belief that there might be a fit between your needs and the foundation's interests, and ask whether it would be appropriate to submit a proposal, including the amount you would be requesting. Making this preliminary contact gets you in front of the foundation (they'll at least know the name of your agency if and when you submit the proposal) and may provide additional information about their priorities that will be helpful as you polish the proposal. If you cannot reach a foundation representative by phone or if your inquiry letter is not answered, submit the proposal anyway.

The Foundation Application

An increasing number of foundations are now requesting online applications — many of which limit the amount of space the writer has in which to make the case for funding. They generally require most of the components requested in the typical written foundation proposal:

- Summary (may not be required online)

- Introduction (may not be required online)

- Problem Statement

- Objectives

- Methods or Proposed Project or Approach

- Evaluation

- Future Funding

- Budget

- Appendices

For a written proposal, you will need a brief cover letter — no more than one page — addressed to the appropriate person at the foundation (the executive director, the program officer, the chair of the grants review committee, or the president). You will know to whom to address the letter from the information you have already gathered in your research. If you are unsure of names, spellings, or whether Jan Anderson is male or female, call the foundation to ask. The cover letter should explain your request — the purpose and the amount you are asking for. If you have already raised some money or received other grants toward this purpose, briefly mention that. Also, reference any earlier contact your agency has made with the foundation. If you or one of your staff has made the contact. the board chair should sign the letter — signifying the board's support of the request.

Sample Cover Letter

Date

Harold Hasalot
Vice President
The Generous Foundation
1234 Dollar Drive
Our Town

Dear Mr. Hasalot:

As a follow-up to our conversation last week, I am submitting the enclosed request for $25,000 to help launch a new literacy program for the parents of the children we serve in our child development center. Nearly half of these individuals have not earned a high school diploma or GED.

To date, we have raised $67,000 from area corporations and individuals toward our goal of $135,000. The board of directors and I sincerely hope that the Foundation will help us provide this much-needed program.

Thank you for your consideration.

Sincerely,

Merry Applicant
Executive Director

enclosure

Summary

The most important part of the proposal is the summary. This is the last part you will write, but it is the first part that will be read. Here is where you hook the reader. The summary has to be compelling — if you lose the reader here, he or she is lost forever, no matter how wonderful the rest of the proposal is.

In writing the summary, go back over the proposal to pick out the main ideas in each section and describe them briefly. Lay out the problem, your proposed solution, the funds needed, and your organization's capacity to solve the problem.

Sample Summary Statement

Child Care Training Association, a 30-year-old United Way affiliate, is submitting this request for $40,000 to support the development and production of a videotape and CD-ROM to provide training on infant and toddler care for entry-level child caregivers in our community.

Who we are; what we are requesting

Today, over half the mothers of infants return to work before their babies' first birthday, and most depend on some form of child care outside of the home. This dramatic new reality is intensified by the critical role a child's earliest experiences play in determining his/her future.

The child care system's response to the new reality has developed along the lines of a consumer service in much the same way, as other businesses have emerged or adapted their services to cater to busy working families. But child care is not simply a consumer service — it is a powerful influence on a young child's life.

Statement of the problem

When children are in care outside of their families, they need to experience close and meaningful attachments to those who care for them. Yet studies document what many parents recognize — child care does not always provide the quality and continuity of care that fosters these attachments.

Child Care Training Association is committed to creating innovative solutions, so that our community's youngest children — who are entrusted to the care of someone other than their parents — have the best possible experiences.

SOur capacity to address the problem

Training is our agency's core competency. We have conducted training for child care providers throughout our area in workshops and seminars, at conferences, through the development of a unique self-guided curriculum and videotape, and through site-by-site consultation and technical assistance.

We are proposing the development and production of two new products which focus on infants and toddlers. The videotape will show a typical day in a high-quality infant/toddler center and how the program is designed to foster attachment. The CD-ROM will allow the user to experience how the physical environment of the infant/toddler center promotes attachment and intimacy.

The proposed project

The success of the project will be evaluated by users' responses to these materials as measured by the number of orders, requests for additional information, user surveys, and feedback from participants in group presentations.

Evaluation

It is our intent that these materials ultimately be self-supporting. The funding we are requesting will pay for development and production, promotion, and 200 copies of each item. The purchase price of the materials will cover that portion of the up-front costs not funded by this grant and all subsequent duplications.

Future funding

Introduction

Start the proposal with a strong introduction, which highlights what your agency is and what you have achieved. Be careful how you describe these achievements. *Our budget has tripled in the last two years* is **not** an achievement — it doesn't tell the reader what you've done. *Tripling the number of parents who read to their children is* an accomplishment.

Accomplishments have to be described in terms of *results* or *outcomes*. The size of your budget or the number of staff hired in the last two years are the *methods* by which you achieved your outcomes — they are not the outcomes themselves. The outcomes describe what happened. What is different as a result of your program? How many parents were enabled to work? How many four-year-olds learned to recognize the letters of the alphabet? How many preschool teachers made observable improvements to their classroom environments?

Sample Introduction

Founded in 1957 by a group of parents, The Chisholm School is an independent, co-educational day school offering preschool through middle school classes to nearly 300 children. We are the only fully accredited, non-sectarian private school in Claridge.

Who we are

Over 70% of our graduates are enrolled in honors classes in their high schools, and a significant number of Chisholm parents are themselves educators — teachers in local public schools and faculty members at our area's four universities.

Evidence of our achievements

Our students represent a diversity of races, religions, and family income levels. Fourteen percent of our students receive financial aid. The school is frequently used for observation by students at area colleges who are preparing to become teachers; our preschool through third grade Montessori classes serve as a learning lab for Montessori programs in this area of the state whose staff are working toward this specialized certification.

Evidence of our credibility

In addition to our outstanding academic programs, we provide extended day activities to meet the needs of working families. With our 90 acres of rolling landscape, lake, and outdoor recreational settings, we also offer a full array of summer camp activities for our students and others in the community.

Responsiveness to the needs of community

Parent involvement is a vital part of the Chisholm experience. Each day, mothers and fathers can be found assisting in the office, library, classrooms, and lunchroom. Special programs such as International Week, Parent Work Days, and various fundraising initiatives rely heavily upon parent participation and support.

Statement reinforces important role of parents — from founding of school to current volunteers

In addition to specific outcomes, present information which establishes your group's credibility. Briefly describe how your organization responds to community needs. Tell what makes your agency unique.

Avoid sweeping statements. *We have always been responsive to the needs of families in our community. Always?* Would that be before or after Columbus discovered America? A statement such as, *Our successful record since our establishment indicates our resourceful and efficient approach to a problem* offers no evidence of success, resourcefulness, or efficiency.

Problem Statement (Statement of Need)

Your problem statement should be direct and to the point. Here is where you use appropriate data (see Chapter 7 for suggestions on data sources) to substantiate the extent of the need. You can use community-wide statistics (*12,000 children are on the waiting list for subsidized child care in our county*) to establish the breadth of the problem. But you're not proposing to serve 12,000 children, so translate that statistic to your neighborhood. *At Community Early Learning Center, we have 300 children on the waiting list.*

Try, wherever possible, to humanize the need. *There are three children waiting for each one of the 100 spaces at the Community Early Learning Center. Their parents are eager to enroll them in our program, so that they can enter public school on an equal footing with children throughout the school district. However, these 300 children and others in years to come will miss this critical opportunity unless we . . .".* That statement evokes more of an image than a mere number.

Use this section to cite research studies or articles in the print media. You can even refer to broadcast media as appropriate — a television reporter has investigated unlicensed child care providers or has done a story on 'latchkey' children. Illustrating the problem with visual images planted in the mind of the reader is always effective. Suggesting urgency is another effective technique — *if we don't address this problem now, here's what will happen* — with a description of what these undesired consequences will be.

The problem that your proposal addresses, while critical, must be reasonable. You must be able to solve it in a reasonable amount of time with a reasonable amount of money. The problem can't be described as so overwhelming that the funder questions whether or not you can solve it.

The need you state is NEVER for money. *Our agency needs $50,000 in order to train 100 low-income women to become teacher aides* is not an appropriate statement of need. *Training 100 low-income women to become teacher aides* is not an appropriate statement of need. *Lifting 100 women out of poverty* will not work as a needs statement, either — there's no way to accomplish that with $50,000.

Your success rests with your definition of a *specific need* among a *targeted group* that you can *realistically meet* by the method you are proposing.

Do not confuse the *need* with the *methods*. A training program for 100 low-income women is a *method* of meeting a need. It is not the need itself. The need is to *increase the supply of trained staff.* Your community needs child care spaces for 750 more children than are currently being served. Facilities are available, but there is a serious shortage of staff.

The proposed training program may not be the only method of meeting the need (for example, you could recruit staff from other parts of the country or you could raid the teacher aide program in the local public schools), but you are suggesting it as the method that will work best — it's the most realistic approach to solving the problem.

Define exactly who will benefit from your proposed project and in what way. If too few people benefit in relation to the level of effort the project will require and the amount of dollars you are requesting, you won't win the grant. But if you expect to change the life of every child in your community, you won't be funded either. No foundation will believe that is possible.

Your proposed project must be seen as adequate to achieve its intended outcomes. If the outcome is *100 newly trained teacher aides will enable 750 more children to be enrolled in early childhood programs in our community*, be sure that $50,000 is an adequate amount to carry out the training. If it's not enough, but it's the foundation's maximum, the proposal should delineate

Sample Problem Statement

The Problem

The foundations of a productive life are laid down in infancy and early childhood.

Simple, declarative statement

The national media have repeatedly spotlighted recent brain research, which demonstrates how children develop the qualities that make them human — language, empathy, and conscience — during the first three years of life. For children at home with their families, these qualities take root in the countless, day-to-day interactions between parent and child.

Credibility borrowed from media; articles could be attached

But for the thousands of small children who spend more of their waking hours in child care than with their parents, these interactions — the cornerstone on which a child's human potential is built — are often missing.

America's youngest children are being cared for in settings in which, according to one national study, only 8.3% of care for babies is considered 'good.' Each hour that a baby in child care is left unattended in a crib or strapped into a swing, each baby bottle propped in a child's mouth, and each cry for comfort that goes unanswered short circuits the 'hard-wiring' of the young child's brain.

Credibility borrowed from study; use of word picture to illustrate problem

Ignoring children's fundamental needs to be cared *about*, not merely cared *for*, has created a crisis of startling proportions — one which, if not addressed, will lead to a generation of children with limited prospects for success in school and later life.

Urgency of problem

---

what part this particular source will play in the total project. What will this $50,000 pay for? Where will the remaining dollars come from?

Is 100 the right number of trainees? Are you sure they will all get jobs? Is there enough program money to pay them decent wages or would they be better off working in fast food restaurants?

Another important consideration is to make sure you are not duplicating what another organization is doing. If the community college is planning a similar training program, you need to show how your project is different or why their program should be augmented by what you are planning. Even better, see if there are ways to collaborate — many foundations favor coordinated approaches.

As noted in Chapter 1, keep children at the center of your proposal — always describing your proposed project in terms of their needs. If you are seeking funds to hire a literacy specialist, it's not because you don't have one. It's because the children need specific activities to help them become ready to read.

Objectives

In this section, you identify the results you intend to achieve. If the problem is a high incidence of child abuse, the objective is not to establish a parent counseling center. The objective is to reduce child abuse.

An objective is always the outcome, the result of the work funded by the grant. Objectives must be measurable; otherwise, how will you know you've achieved them? An objective can be stated as an increase in some desirable condition or as a decrease in some undesirable condition — either of which are measurable.

Establishing a parent counseling center is not an objective — it is a method. Methods or activities are never objectives. Objectives are *what* you want to have happen as a result of the grant. Methods or activities tell *how* it will happen.

In writing objectives, many grant writers follow the acronym **SMART**. Objectives must be **Specific, Measurable, Achievable, Realistic**, and **Time-framed**. Because that acronym is so widely used, you can assume that the foundation staff who review your proposal are likely to apply it as well.

Methods (Approach)

Not only do the methods have to relate to the problem and the objectives, there needs to be a good explanation of why these particular methods have

Sample Objectives

The proposed project is a 20-week training program for 30 child care center directors and 15 River County Social Services Department staff to help them increase their knowledge of child growth and development and child care center administration. The program features weekly seminars, with self-teaching guidebooks, presentations by trainers, group discussions, and role playing designed to bridge the gap between theory and practice.

*Seminars, group discussions, role playing, etc., are **not** objectives; they are activities.*

Objectives

The training program will meet the following objectives:

1. By week 12 of the training, 45 trainees will demonstrate increased knowledge of child growth and development as evidenced by pre- and post-written descriptions of typical developmental characteristics of preschool-age children.

2. By week 12 of the training, 45 trainees will identify the components of an effective program to meet the intellectual, social, emotional, and physical needs of young children, as measured by trainees' pre- and post-evaluation of a daily schedule of appropriate activities.

3. By week 15 of the training, the 30 center directors will show increased proficiency from pre- to post-test in analyzing case studies focusing on effective guidance of children with behavioral difficulties.

What do we want to have happen?
- *number of trainees*
- *what they will gain*
- *how we will know what they gained*

4. By week 15 of the training, the 30 center directors will demonstrate increased ability to identify characteristics of children with special needs and to determine appropriate programming as measured by pre- and post-analyses of case studies.

5. By week 20, 45 trainees will increase their ability to describe the roles and responsibilities of staff, board, and parents, and to delineate decision-making processes as evidenced by pre- and post-analyses of case studies.

6. By week 20, 45 trainees will improve their ability to develop program policies to guide the daily operations of child care centers, as measured by their pre- and post-analyses of situations requiring problem-solving skills and policy enactments.

been chosen. Sometimes methods are self-evident, like building a new facility to replace an aging structure. But other problems often have multiple possible solutions. Why are you choosing one program model over another? What leads you to believe that your proposed alternative will work best?

In this section, give the foundation a realistic picture of how its money will be spent. Describe who will be served, how many will be served, how they will be served, and for what period of time. Set out a sequence of activities: What will happen when? How will participants be recruited? Describe the staffing needed to carry out the program or project. This should include all relevant positions — new and current, the qualifications for these positions, and the key responsibilities of each. Explain any unique features of the program or project.

If you have already completed initial planning for your project (securing other agencies to partner with you, hiring an architect, conducting research), be sure to mention this preliminary work as part of your approach.

Evaluation

Well-defined objectives will tell you what to evaluate. Did you accomplish what you intended to? Did you get the results you expected? What are the outcomes? What changes occurred as a result of the grant?

You will not only want to measure achievement of your objectives, you will want to know how successful your methods were. What activities worked best? Did you have to make any mid-course corrections?

Specify who will do the evaluation. If it is your staff, describe how you will make sure that the evaluation is objective and unbiased.

Build in specific measurement criteria by defining success measures. Don't be afraid to aim high on measures you can control. In baseball, the best hitters get a hit only three to four times out of ten tries — they have a 30%

to 40% success rate. But what child care program would define success as 80% of the children going home with the right parent at the end of the day? Or even 99%? If you're going to ask for money to accomplish something meaningful, you'd better be able to influence the outcome to a significant degree. If not, what's the point?

That said, if you reduced child abuse by 100% among the families who attended the programs at your parent counseling center, but you lost 75% of the participants in the first two months, a foundation might question the success of the program. Perhaps for this population, 25% retention in the program *is* success. If so, define it as such in your objectives, recognizing that you can't control many of the factors that contribute to family instability.

Describe when and how you will collect your evaluation data — interviews, behavioral observations, reviews of records, pre-/post-assessments, etc. Bear in mind that data collection does not take place only at the end of the project. Start implementing the evaluation at the outset — gathering whatever baseline information will be compared against the participants' progress, as well as the project's outcomes. It is much easier to collect data as you go along than to backtrack when it's time to complete the evaluation.

Future Funding

Most foundations will want you to describe how you are going to continue your program once their grant dollars have been spent. The *ideal* plan for future funding is that you won't need any — the grant will start you off and then the program will become self-supporting or will be adopted by another, more permanent funding source, or you will have solved the problem addressed by the grant once and for all. However, that's not likely to be the case.

Even if you submit a grant request for a one-time equipment purchase or remodeling of your facility, you will have ongoing maintenance, repair, and operating costs. For example, in considering your request for funds to purchase a bus, a foundation should know how you plan to pay for insurance, license plates, gasoline, and future repairs.

Avoid vague statements such as, *We will make a determined attempt to seek other funds*. Instead, present a plan that sounds possible to achieve. Perhaps you will charge a fee for services, develop a publication to be sold, or have an annual event that will support this program, or maybe the program will be funded by your local United Way once you've been able to demonstrate its success with the initial grant funding. Are there likely to be new sources of government funding for the program — at the local, state, or federal levels? Will you investigate collaboration with another program that might bring dollars to the table? Point out the major milestones that the board has committed to in your fund development plan. If you will be inaugurating an annual direct mail campaign or starting an auxiliary group of 'friends' whose membership contributions will be a source of ongoing support, describe these initiatives, along with how much you expect to raise each year.

A foundation won't expect a guarantee of future funding, but it will expect a plan that has been thought through and is appropriate for your organization.

If you are seeking additional funds for the project from other sources, mention that in the proposal. Don't just throw together a list of foundations you think you might apply to — do your homework. Discuss which specific sources you believe might fund your project.

Budget

The budget is one proposal section that can be laden with pitfalls. In addition to no calculation errors, there should be no surprises. The budget has to agree with the rest of the proposal. This is not the place to show four salaries when only one staff position has been mentioned in the proposal narrative . . . or to budget only minimum wage for a position that has been described in the proposal as key to the project.

Errors can occur when the financial person in an organization works on the proposal budget, while the program person is developing the proposal narrative, and they don't come together until the end of the process. Or mistakes are made because the financial staff has to wait until the proposal narrative is complete before they can build the budget, and they have to hustle to meet the submission deadline.

A better way to work is to define what the program or project is going to look like, expense-wise, as part of the initial proposal development — *before* the narrative is written. How many new positions will be needed? What existing positions will be allocated to the program? At what percentages? What other expenses are required? This enables the budget preparer to be working while the grant writer is preparing the narrative.

The grant writer tells the story in words; the budget preparer tells the story in dollars and cents. They must tell the same story — the budget must reflect the narrative and the narrative has to agree with the budget. If there's a line item in the budget for a bus, the narrative should explain what the bus will be used for, who will drive it, how it will enhance the program, and how it contributes to the desired outcomes. Similarly, any significant item in the narrative — staff performance incentives, staff development activities, new staff — must be addressed in the budget.

The budget should raise no questions. It should be detailed and specific. Rounding a line item to the nearest thousand won't help your credibility. Round to the nearest dollar, or ten, at the most. Be careful with the line item for *miscellaneous expenses*. Keep it to a limited amount and give parenthetical examples of what might be included.

Use *real* numbers, not *this sounds about right* estimates. Budgets that are obviously padded or that are clearly insufficient to do the job can sink an otherwise excellent proposal.

If the foundation has its own budget forms or specifies budget categories, follow these. If not, you can use something similar to the budget format on the next page, keeping in mind that a construction budget will have different line items, direct services to children will require a larger personnel budget, and a one-time equipment purchase will show only a few line items.

Sample Project Budget

Project Personnel		$100,650
Executive Director — .2 FTE		
$75,000 @ 20%	15,000	
Parent Educator — 1.0 FTE	50,000	
Administrative Assistant		
— .5 FTE		
$35,000 @ 50%	17,500	
Sub-Total	82,500	
Benefits and Payroll Taxes		
22% of salaries	18,150	

Show the percentage of time that each person who will be paid partially by the grant will be devoting to the project.

Printing		$ 9,100
5,000 brochures @ $1.62	8,100	
5,000 envelopes @ .20	1,000	

Itemize the expenditures for which you have exact figures (number of units and cost per unit).

Postage		$ 2,850
5,000 @ .57		

Office Equipment & Supplies		$ 2,000
Laptop computer	1,500	
Inkjet printer	300	
Replacement cartridges	100	
Desk supplies (paper,		
pens, etc.)	100	

Use exact costs for equipment purchases; supply costs can be estimated.

Meeting Space		$ 2,750
Monthly rental @ $250 x 11 months		
Refreshments		$ 1,375
11 events @ $125		
Total Request		$118,725

FTE = Full-Time Equivalent or Full-Time Employee

Appendices

Most foundations will tell you what they want you to attach to your proposal, but sometimes you have to guess. Generally, expect to provide:

- your 501(c)(3) determination letter from the IRS

- a list of your board of directors, with their affiliations (who they work for and their titles — for board members who don't work, designate them as *community volunteers*)

- your most recent audited financial statement

Some foundations may also request your articles of incorporation, your agency's annual operating budget, an organization chart, and a list of other supporters. Unless the foundation stipulates otherwise, you might send one or more of the more persuasive items in your credibility file. Select those items that lend the best support to the proposal — perhaps a recent newspaper article or a testimonial letter.

CHAPTER 7

Preparing Government Grant Applications: Dear Mr. Bureaucrat

Receiving government funding can feel like hitting the jackpot. The commitment is often multi-year or open-ended. The dollar amounts are usually substantial, and your agency's credibility will be significantly increased in the eyes of other funders.

But the application process can be overwhelming, requiring a great deal of detailed information submitted in a prescribed format. The deadline may be as short as four weeks, sometimes less. Government grants are even more competitive than foundation funding, attracting highly competent organizations with the capacity not only to deliver the program to be funded, but also to submit high-scoring applications. And government funding comes with strings attached — some of which can tie your program up in knots.

Before you apply for government funding, whether it is through a grant process or the submission of vendor forms in order to be eligible to participate in a child care voucher program, be sure your organization has a strong accounting function. Scattered receipts and mis-filed records won't do. When you accept public funds, you are accepting the public trust. Your organization must have the capacity to track government funds as they are received, report on how they are spent, and adhere to the policies governing the expenditure of these dollars. In child care voucher programs, keeping accurate enrollment, attendance records, and documentation of parent fee payments is crucial. Grant or contract awards have more complex requirements. They may mandate competitive procurement — you will have to put the purchase of some items out for bid, rather than just doing business with the same vendor(s) you have worked with in the past. There may be limits on how much you can spend on conference travel, with hotel rates and meal allowances specified by location and receipts required for reimbursement. Certain expenses (such as refreshments for parent meetings) may not be permitted. So weigh carefully the costs of doing business with the government.

This chapter features a sample Early Head Start application. Since most federal grants follow the same format with similar proposal sections, evaluation criteria, etc., this model can serve as a guideline for other federal funding sources. However, it is only a guideline — not a template. Federal applications can and do change over time. State funding applications may be equally detailed or less complex, depending upon the agency and whether the application is for federal funds administered by the state or for a state-funded program with its own criteria.

If you're going to apply, you need to get organized. This will definitely be a team effort.

Organizing for the Task

Before you begin writing the proposal, read the application thoroughly. If you have submitted a previous application for these funds in response to an earlier announcement, don't assume because this year's application package looks like last year's, that they are the same. Some sections of the new application may be in a different order or there may be new requirements that you have to address. Also, look carefully at the review criteria — although you will follow the application's outline, it is these criteria that you must attend to, since that is how your application will be scored.

Make a copy of the program announcement or request for proposal for everyone who has a need to know about it, especially those staff members who will be contributing to the development of the proposal. If you want to save paper and you have the time to divide the announcement into sections, you might give just the budget section to your financial person, the section on staffing to whoever handles human resources issues, and so forth, but be sure that everyone has what is relevant to them — even if it's spread among several sections.

Set some deadlines. It's helpful to have three deadlines, backing up from the date the proposal has to leave your site in order to arrive at its destination on time. It must arrive on time — government agencies will not accept late submissions, even if you hand it to the overnight delivery company in time to meet the deadline and the company failed to get it there as promised.

If the proposal has to be received on Monday, for example, it must leave your site no later than the preceding Friday (deadline #3) for overnight delivery. You should allow one day for any last minute changes, and to make and assemble the copies. Thus, the final draft has to be finished on Wednesday (deadline #2), so final changes and copies can be made Thursday. In order to finish the final draft, you need everyone's contributions no later than the previous Wednesday (deadline #1) or earlier, if possible.

Sample Calendar

Sun	Monday	Tuesday	Wednesday	Thursday	Friday	Sat
			1	2	3	4
						5
6	7	8	9 **(1) All proposal sections due**	10 Work on final draft	11 Work on final draft	12
13	14 Work on final draft	15 Work on final draft	16 **(2) Final draft completed**	17 Last minute changes; copying	18 **(3) Proposal to delivery company**	19
20	21 **PROPOSAL DEADLINE**	22	23	24	25	26
27	28	29	30	31		

Everyone involved in the proposal submission process, including the board chair — if his or her signature or a board resolution is required, must be aware of the deadlines and commit to meeting them.

Consider using an assignment form which breaks the application down into its components and identifies who is responsible for which parts.

Sample Assignment Form

Early Head Start Proposal

Due:_____ Out:_____ To (Final Editor): _____
(Deadline)   (Mailing Date)   (Date)

Objectives and Need for Assistance	Assigned to:
Data to be gathered:	
Birth rates in targeted ZIP codes	
# of children 0-3 in targeted ZIP codes	
# of teen parents in targeted ZIP codes	
% of teen parents receiving prenatal care and when (first, second, third trimester)	
unemployment rate in community	
# households in target area with at least one member employed	
# families on TANF in targeted ZIP codes	
household income in targeted ZIP codes	
# or % of minority and non-English speaking families in target area	
# 0-3 on waiting list for child care subsidies in targeted ZIP codes	
# subsidized care providers serving 0-3 in targeted ZIP codes; # of vacancies	
# of children on waiting list for our agency's services in target area	
# abuse/neglect referrals in targeted ZIP codes	
# of families enrolled in WIC	
# children in ECI program	
map of target areas	
# and type of programs serving 0-3 child care and others; programs serving pregnant women in targeted ZIP codes	
# of NAEYC, NAFCC accredited programs in target area	

Results or Benefits Expected	Assigned to:
Benefits resulting from collaborative partnerships	
Qualitative and quantitative data to measure progress toward results	
How will program know it achieved its objectives?	
Description of how we currently/will collect data on families	

Approach	Assigned to:
Action plan (scope and detail)	
Reasons for proposed approach	
Monthly or quarterly projections of accomplishments for each function or activity	
How stakeholders in community will be involved	
Recruitment and selection of participants	
Child development services	
Transition to other programs at age 3	
Provision of well-baby/well-child health care	
Procedures for individualized family partnership agreements	
Promoting adult and family health and wellness	
Promoting progress toward economic self-sufficiency	
Assistance on income support, child support, related assistance	
Existing or planned transportation resources for accessing needed services	

Note that the section assignments are very specific. One person can be responsible for all the assignments in one section, or you may wish to assign different pieces of one section to a team of individuals, or you might just assign one specialized task to someone. If some of these people write well, you'll probably be able to use what they produce with only minor edits. Don't let your team become immobilized because they don't think they can write well enough.

What is important is that they get you (or whoever is writing the proposal) the information.

Give each team member a copy of the forms with his or her assignment(s) highlighted. If your computer system is networked, create a shared directory, so each person can enter his or her pieces of the proposal. Make sure they name their files to reflect the section they are working on. Once you have read and edited their contributions, copy each file into a master proposal file or folder. Number each draft to avoid confusion about which is the current version.

Staff and Position Data	Assigned to:
Biographical sketch for each key person	
Job description for each vacant key position	

Organization Profile	Assigned to:
Organization chart	
Financial statements, audits, EIN, non-profit status	
Child care licenses and NAEYC accreditation	
Info on compliance with government standards	
Experience in the program area: • management of comprehensive services • management of community, state, and federal partnerships • history and relationship with target community • program's financial status • program operations • how program data will be collected and analyzed • automated information systems for continuous improvement • maintenance of confidentiality	
Organizational structure	
Staff development approach and rationale	
Key management activities during start-up	
Corporate capacity within service area: • type of agency, years of experience • organizational structure • types of services provided • population and numbers served • overall agency budget • presence in service area (relationships and activities)	

Collaboration	Assigned to:
Interagency agreements	

Letters of Support	Assigned to:
Provide samples — different letter for each: • United Way • licensing department • Early Childhood Intervention • city council • workforce development board • business leaders • program advisory board • principal of local high school • others	

Budget	Assigned to:
One-time start-up costs	
Narrative	
Non-federal share	
Costs of renovation to comply with Performance Standards	
Appropriateness of compensation and funding for staff development	
Travel	

In addition to what your staff will contribute to the proposal, you will need three critical inputs from outside resources: data, inter-agency agreements, and letters of support. Since you are depending on outsiders whose schedules you don't control, you have to get that ball rolling as early as possible. Assign the collection of these pieces first — preferably to someone on your team who is persistent, tenacious, and charming.

Keep a master copy of the forms showing everyone's assignments. It's helpful to have these forms in a binder, with a section for each person who is contributing to the proposal. Insert a copy of each person's assignments into his/her section. As they complete their assignments, place a hard copy of their work in their sections of the notebook, along with any back-up data, copies of letters or e-mails they have written to others requesting information, etc. Having each person submit a hard copy of their work is essential, since there is always the chance that a file they've saved in the computer won't make it into the final document, because its name is similar to another file, it was mis-named, the editing process was interrupted, someone accidentally deleted the file, their computer crashed, or the network went down.

If you keep all of this material, by the end of the proposal process, you will have a complete notebook to use for reference in program-planning and for future grant applications. More important, a well-organized process insures that the application can go forward in the absence of a key individual or when some other crisis looms.

Where to Find the Data You Need

The first part of the assignment form on page 85 shows some of the data to present in describing the need. Make sure your data are narrowed down for your proposed service area(s), rather than descriptive of the state, city, or community at large. In an Early Head Start proposal, you'll need information on the number of children ages 0-3. For a pre-K or Head Start proposal, use the number of children ages 0-5, or, if you can get it, ages 3-5. Sometimes you may have to extrapolate. For example, census statistics do not break down the number of 3- to 5-year-olds, but health department data on the number of live births three, four, and five years ago will approximate the size of that population.

Census data (**http://QuickFacts.Census.gov** or **www.Census.gov**) are useful for general population, income, ethnicity, education, employment, and other family statistics.

Your local health department can give you data on birth rates, births to teens, women receiving prenatal care, and WIC participants.

Children's Protective Services (CPS) can give you data on abuse and neglect cases.

Part C or ECI agencies have information on children with delays or developmental disabilities.

The local child care subsidy management program or child care resource and referral agency should be able to give you information on the number of children on the waiting list for subsidized child care, the number of available child care spaces, and the accreditation status of the programs.

Some of the data you need are available on the Internet. Or, you may have to identify contacts in the appropriate public agencies and coax the information out of them. It's worth whatever effort is involved to secure data that make a compelling case for your proposal. A sample contact log is provided below.

Remember to write a thank-you note to anyone who provided information — they'll remember that when you ask them for help again next time. Or they'll remember that you didn't send one.

Also, send a thank-you note to anyone who writes a letter of support. If you do get the grant, write or call anyone who provided data or who wrote a letter of support to tell them the good news and to thank them once more for their help.

Sample Data Collection Log

Organization	Contact Person	Phone or e-mail	Information Requested	Date Rec'd	Date Thank You Sent

Writing the Proposal

Government grant applications usually have page limits. In determining how much to write, a good rule of thumb is to allocate pages according to the number of points you could earn for any single section. If the section on "Objectives and Need for Assistance" is worth 15 points out of 100 (15%), then you could reasonably devote 7-8 pages to this section in a 50-page proposal or about 11 pages in a 75-page document.

Objectives and Need for Assistance

In this section, you are asked to 'make the case' for your proposed program: demonstrate the need (who, what, and where) and define relevant objectives. The need should be thoroughly documented by statistics, using the most current data you have found. The objectives should relate to addressing the need.

Example

Background
The majority of mothers of young children in Maple County
— regardless of income — are working or preparing for
work, and that is not expected to change in the foreseeable
future:

- Mapleview, the county seat, is the fastest-growing
  population center in the Midwest, with a growth
  rate more than twice the national average.
- Maple County is among the top three counties in
  the tri-state area in job growth, having added 9,372
  jobs from 1990 to 2000.
- While the statewide unemployment rate is currently
  6.9%, the unemployment rate in Maple County is
  5.4%.

Economic data highlight target area compared to nation, region, rest of state

Even with the uncertainties of the current economy,
Mapleview has an abundance of service jobs, the traditional
gateway to the workforce for individuals with limited job

skills and experience. For families who could benefit from Early Head Start, it is the unavailability of appropriate full-day child care that consigns them to continuing poverty.

Objectives

The objectives for the proposed Early Head Start program are derived from assessments of community needs by a variety of entities, including Greater Mapleview Head Start, United Way of Maple County, Maple County Workforce Development Board, Mapleview Child Care Resource and Referral, and the Maple County Department of Health and Human Services. These assessments indicate a number of pressing problems:

- more than 1,100 births to teens aged 13-17 every year

- one in three 2-year-olds not fully immunized

- an average of 750 confirmed cases of child abuse and neglect every year

- 17,000 children living in poverty

- child-care licensing standards among the lowest in the country.

Sources of assessment data; key findings

The proposed program is a step toward solving these problems in an area not currently served by Early Head Start.

Child Development Objectives

1. 60 children will benefit from full-day, comprehensive child development services in a facility designed especially for children 0-3
Additional objectives related to this heading

Each major program component has its own objectives

Family Development Objectives

2. Teen parents, both mothers and fathers, will experience success in parenting and will complete high school
Additional objectives related to this heading

Community-Wide Objectives
3. Youth in the community will contribute to the Early Head Start program
Additional objectives related to this heading

Staff Development Objectives
4. Staff will achieve educational benchmarks required by Head Start Performance Standards
Additional objectives related to this heading

Population to be Served
The program is designed to serve eligible parents who are working, participating in training, or attending school. The maximum number of individuals to be served is 68; the maximum number of children in care at any one time is 60; the maximum number of pregnant women is eight.

Of the 60 children, 30 will be up to 18 months (infants) and 30 between the ages of 18 months and three years old (toddlers). The 30 infant spaces include those reserved for the babies of pregnant women, so the mothers can be assured of child care when they are ready to return to work, training, or school after childbirth.

Geographic Location
The Early Head Start program will be delivered in ZIP code 00000, a community with a demonstrated need for the services to be provided, but with no Early Head Start programs. The nearest Early Head Start program is in Elm County at a facility 34 miles away.

The proposed site is at the corner of Main Street and Fourth Avenue in Mapleview. A detailed map is attached as Appendix I.

The ZIP code in which the program will be located has a large minority population. Although 91% of the families have at least one member employed, more than 20% of the families within the target area have incomes below $15,000.

The area is home to over 1,100 children under age 3, 246 TANF recipients, and 982 WIC clients. Health department

Each major program component has its own objectives

Target population: who and how many

Verification of unserved population

Specific location

Characteristics of community which validate the need

data indicate 134 births in the last year to teens living there. Forty-four percent of these mothers received no prenatal care until at least the second trimester of their pregnancies, including 20% who had no care until their sixth month or later.

Although there are various social services and health care providers in the area, their services are not currently integrated on behalf of pregnant women or young children.

Documentation of lack of resources

Within the ZIP code, there are 6 child care centers that participate in the child care subsidy system. Only 15% of their capacity is licensed for children under age 3.

In addition to the statistics that you include in the section on need, try to prepare a brief description of the community that gives the grant reviewer(s) a feel for what life is like there every day and why your proposed program would make a difference. As early childhood professionals often say, "Use your words" to paint a picture of what the community looks like.

Here are a few examples:

Mapleview is the ninth largest city in the state and one of the 100 largest cities in the U.S. The proposed program site is in the city's lowest income area. It is close to bus routes on Mapleview's main thoroughfare. Mapleview is served by six major highways, providing residents with linkages to jobs throughout the region. Public transportation services were recently enhanced with the arrival of light rail.

Mapleview's strengths relate to its industrial base and commitment to growth. Over 4,500 businesses operate in the city. Both the public and private sectors are strongly committed to job creation and commercial growth. The city offers an attractive incentive package to businesses considering relocation, as well as programs geared to resident industries. The community's strong business base has helped provide solid financial support for the school system.

Mapleview's pride in its business base is a community strength — a factor which is addressed in the proposal review process. Moreover, the availability of jobs helps make the case for a full-day, full-year Early Head Start program to help families who are seeking to become more self-sufficient. This type of information usually can be found on the web sites of cities and Chambers of Commerce.

> North Oakton has the feel of a small, rural town — even though it lies directly across the Grafton River from downtown Central City. It is a tree-filled, hilly, residential community with unparalleled views of the urban skyline. It is bi-sected by Interstate 49, which runs north/south and is bounded on the north by Interstate 61, the main east/west highway between Central City and Clarkston. One of the proposed expansion sites lies near the apex of these two major roads; the other is closer to the I-49 corridor. Both are a short ride from downtown.

> Madison Boulevard, a main thoroughfare, runs east and west through North Oakton. It is lined by historic structures now converted to taquerias, thrift stores, and other retail establishments. The boulevard links the two proposed Early Head Start sites. The church is on one end, the existing child development center is further west, two blocks south of Madison.

The description of North Oakton could be produced from a drive through the neighborhood.

Adding a little local color or history, where appropriate, is likely to engage the reviewer. In addressing the strengths of the Mapleview community, the focus was on its business base. For North Oakton, the emphasis is on community stability.

> The strengths of the North Oakton community relate to its history and infrastructure. The Oakton United Community Church, one of the proposed Early Head Start sites, was established in 1887. Despite a tornado in 1894 (reducing the structure to a "mass of kindling wood," according to church documents), and a fire in 1958, the church has remained deeply rooted in the community.

Any applicant should be able to earn the full 15 points for the section on "Objectives and Need for Assistance." Further, since this is the first section that's read, if it's done well, it sets the tone for the rest of the proposal.

Check your work:

Are the data you've provided specific? You can't simply say that Mapleview is a low-income community with many underserved children. That's true, but it requires documentation.

Have you cited the statistics that best relate to your proposed program? Domestic violence, hunger among the elderly, and inadequate shelters for the homeless may be pressing problems in your community. But unless they directly relate to your proposal — even if they relate indirectly — don't include them. There's no point in cluttering the proposal with every societal ill — address only the problem you are trying to solve.

In the same vein, what are the factors in your community that you can point to in order to make the case for the need for your proposed program (e.g., new job creation, expanded training programs for adults, construction of low-income housing, the annual influx of seasonal or migrant workers, etc.)? Are your statistics up to date? If not, don't use them. Don't taint your credibility with numbers that no longer apply.

Have you spelled out your objectives as precisely as possible? Did you state *what* you want to have happen, not *how* it will happen?

Results or Benefits Expected

This section asks you to define the specific results or benefits the participants (including other community agencies) will gain from your program, describe the data you will collect, and tell how you will use funding for continuous improvement.

The specific results or benefits must be related to the objectives you have already described. The objectives tell *what* you intend to accomplish; the results or benefits tell *why*. The data collection tells how you'll know the objective has been achieved.

Are the results and benefits of your proposed program stated concretely and do they link to the objectives? What's the benefit to children and families if these objectives are achieved? Why are these objectives meaningful? This explanation is critical — it's what gives your proposal integrity.

When you are ready to prepare this section of the proposal, review each objective you have identified. For each one, jot down *key* words that tell:

- what (*what you want to have happen*)

- why (*why it is important*)

- how (*how you will measure whether it happened*)

Then, write.

You must also describe how you will use the data you collect to measure your progress in achieving your objectives and to make adjustments or improvements where needed. Think about what it is you are planning to do and what information would tell you if you've done it, how well you are doing it, or if you need to do something else. The reason for data collection in any field is to gain information that leads to better decisions, improved services, innovative products. Whether it's a new prescription drug or a method of teaching reading, the idea is to find out what works or doesn't work.

In preparing this section, consider to whom you will report progress in meeting objectives (your board of directors, parent policy council, others), how often progress reports will be made (monthly, quarterly, other), how you will set benchmarks for accomplishment of objectives (annual planning session, quarterly reviews, other), and what you will do if objectives are not being met (re-prioritize work, re-design procedures, re-train staff).

Examples

Benefits Related to Objective 1
(indicate on which page this objective appears)
Sixty infants and toddlers in low-income families in which parents are striving to become self-sufficient will have access to an early care and education program that will foster their optimal growth and development, while meeting their parents' needs for affordable substitute care arrangements.

Outcome Data
Quantitative
- number of infants and toddlers served
- enrollment and attendance rates
- number of parents employed, in training, or in school

Benefits Related to Objective 2
(indicate on which page this objective appears)
Teen parents will be supported in overcoming the special challenges that face them, so they are better prepared for adulthood. The babies of teen parents will have a greater chance of healthy development.

Outcome Data
Quantitative
- number of teen parents staying in or completing high school during their participation in program
- number of teen parents actively involved in program
- number of teen fathers involved in program

Qualitative
- comparison of developmental and health assessments of children of teen parents with those of older parents currently served by Early Head Start
- observations of parent/child interactions indicating healthy relationships

The benefits of the full-day, comprehensive child development program are: parent self-sufficiency, optimal growth and development of children, affordable child care

These and the following objectives lend themselves to both quantitative and qualitative measures

98

**Benefits Related to Objective 3
(indicate on which page this objective appears)**
Youth in the community will develop a sense of being valued, of mattering, and of making a real difference in the lives of others.

Outcome Data
Quantitative
- number of opportunities for community youth participation
- number of youths participating in Early Head Start activities and events

Qualitative
- evidence of youth attachment to community institutions such as the Early Head Start program
- observable instances of other civic engagement by youth
- evaluations by youth of their participation in Early Head Start

**Benefits Related to Objective 4
(indicate on which page this objective appears)**
Staff will participate in educational opportunities to improve their knowledge and skills in working with infants, toddlers, and their families. Staff will receive salary increases for educational attainment ranging from $250 to $1,500, depending on the level of achievement.

Outcome Data
Qualitative
- number of staff achieving Child Development Associate credential, two-year, or four-year degrees in related fields
- number of outside training hours earned by staff

Quantitative
- results of individual performance reviews

Approach

This is the heart of the application, worth the most points and the most effort on your part. Be sure to fully address each item requested and lay out your action plan, step by step.

Here you describe why you have chosen your approach, how it follows best practices, and exactly what your plan of action is. This section should demonstrate your understanding and depth of knowledge of your profession. For a program of direct service to children, pay particular attention to your discussion of child development and child care. For instance, it is not enough to cite a particular curriculum you plan to use and quote from it in describing your approach. Any curriculum is only a resource for the program design, it is not the program design itself.

Examples

Introduction

The proposed approach is to offer Early Head Start services to families who currently have or will soon have a need for child care, with child care as the keystone of the entire program rather than as a support service delivered by other providers. This approach has three unique aspects:

1. Every pregnant woman enrolled will be guaranteed a child care space in the program when she is ready for it. She will be considered a 'child care client' even before her baby is born and will be invited to participate in all of the parent activities offered by the program.

2. The program will be carefully designed to address the risks to the parent/child relationship that emerge when infants and toddlers spend more of their time in the care of others than with their own families.

3. The center will offer Head Start/child care services for preschool-age siblings of the Early Head Start children, reinforcing the bridge between the home and the program.

Emphasizes this particular approach for this population (parents who need child care, because they are working or are in school/ training)

Recruitment of Families

Early Head Start staff will aggressively recruit low-income, pregnant women and families with infants and toddlers for the program. We will work with other agencies that provide services to low-income families, especially those serving recent immigrants, non-English-speaking people, and families receiving — or at risk of receiving — TANF, who are targeted by welfare-to-work programs. Close communication already exists with many of these organizations and new linkages will be developed where appropriate.

Examples of recruitment strategies include outreach through the following:

- WIC and other public agencies serving low-income, pregnant women or families with infants and toddlers
- Health service providers, including hospitals and community clients
- ECI and other services for children under 3 with developmental delays or disabilities
- Local high schools
- The Salvation Army, homeless shelters, food pantries
  Additional agencies

Pre-Literacy and Language

Pre-literacy is a key component of our programs. The approach is based on the following principles:

- The foundation for literacy begins in the very early years.
- When babies and toddlers are around adults who value and take pleasure in books and reading, they develop book-handling behaviors, story-reading behaviors, and, eventually, a love of books.
  — With exposure, babies and toddlers become easily engaged with books and want to assist with 'reading' the pictures and words.
  — An early literacy program involves activities for the parents at home, as well as activities for the children at the center.

Specific descriptions of target populations, agencies to be contacted

The pre-literacy program is based on established principles, which are then translated into specific practices

Our pre-literacy program promotes and supports early literacy with activities that address staff and parents, along with children:

Staff

1. Staff talk to the babies and toddlers during routines and activities.

2. Staff repeat the sounds that babies make and add to the words that toddlers say.

3. Staff read daily to the children: one on one or in a small group.
   Additional examples

Parents

1. Parents are introduced to the use of the public library and are encouraged to obtain library cards.

2. Parents are notified of a local retailer's giveaway of free books.

3. Parents are given opportunities to improve their literacy skills through planned program activities and referrals to community adult literacy programs.
   Additional examples

Children

1. Children are encouraged to vocalize, talk, and sing.

2. Books are accessible, so children can handle them.

3. Books and printed materials represent the children's cultural and linguistic backgrounds.
   Additional examples

Specific examples of how staff promote pre-literacy

Specific examples of how parents are involved

Specific examples of how children experience pre-literacy

Organizational Profiles/ Staff and Position Data

This is the section in which you demonstrate your agency's capability, competence, and credibility. Here is where you sell, sell, sell. What has your organization accomplished that makes you worthy of this grant? If you don't have a *lot* to point to, make the most of what you *have* done. If key individuals are new to your agency and don't have early childhood, Head Start, or grants management experience, be creative in relating the experience they do have to your program. "Being creative" doesn't mean falsifying or exaggerating. It just means finding and highlighting relevant connections.

Be specific as to the skills of the various members of your management team. What is their fiscal expertise? What experience have they had working with other community organizations?

Example

Management of Comprehensive Services and Partnerships

Throughout the years since our founding, our agency has developed and managed innovative services to meet the changing needs of children and their families. Many of our programs have involved city, state, and federal partnerships, as follows:

1994 — We were selected by the local housing authority to develop and manage a network of family child care homes within the city's largest housing project.

1997 — We received a $503,712, U.S. Department of Labor contract to recruit, hire, and train 99 unemployed individuals as child care workers.

2000 — We were the successful bidder for management of the state's child care subsidy program in our county. We currently manage over $40 million in annual subsidies.

2002 — We were selected by the state employment commission as one of only two grantees statewide in the Micro-Enterprise Development Program. Our $421,800 grant enabled us to assist welfare recipients in becoming family child care providers.

The programs cited represent examples of federal, state, and local partnerships

They demonstrate the agency's breadth of experience (family child care, voucher management, training)

They also indicate experience managing grants and contracts of significant size

Staff Development Approach and Rationale

Our agency's staff development plan is an integral part of assuring program excellence. Its aim is to help staff develop a sense of themselves as competent individuals. Staff development plans relate to the position, as well as to the individual. Professional development opportunities are varied and planned with staff input. Training is ongoing and unlimited.

Staff development activities will include:
- pre-service orientation and training
- plans to obtain professional credentials, certifications, and degrees
- regularly scheduled training sessions
- presentations by program consultants
- attendance at local, state, and national conferences.

Staff development is tied to program quality; it has a definable, measurable goal and it is individualized

Specific examples are listed

Be sure that the staffing pattern you describe (positions and reporting relationships) supports the program you propose (see form below).

Proposed Staffing Pattern

Position	FTE	Reports To	Comments

The application requires a biographical sketch for each key staff member. A biographical sketch is not a resumé — it is a narrative description highlighting the individual's skills and experience.

Example

Social Services Manager
Connie Velasquez graduated from Local College with a B.S. degree in Human Development and earned her MSW from State University. She has over eight years of experience in social services, including three years as program coordinator and manager for Metro Homeless Services, where she provided outreach, crisis intervention, and assessments for homeless youth and families. As a clinician, Ms. Velasquez coordinated client services with local community social services agencies. She began her career with our agency as a resource and referral counselor, helping families obtain child care and other needed services. She has been in her current position for the last two years.

Ms. Velasquez has volunteered with the Department of Human Services Child Abuse Unit and is past president of the Maple City Association for Infant Mental Health. She is currently program chair of the Maple City Association for the Education of Young Children, and a member of the Early Childhood Consortium and the state Head Start association.

Focus is on education and professional experience

Volunteer activities as a professional are included

No hobbies, church activities, or social clubs are mentioned

If resumés are requested, don't submit the resumés already in your files — the ones that your staff used when they first applied for the job. These resumés are not up to date. They won't include the current positions — the very ones you need to highlight. They also may not include additional education each person has attained while working for you or any leadership positions she or he has been appointed or elected to in professional organizations. Moreover, resumé styles vary from person to person. It looks much better if all resumés submitted with the application are in the same format. If you have 10 resumés to attach and they all look different, the quickest way to unify them is to create a standard format, give each of the 10 people a copy or computer template, and ask them to revise and update their resumés accordingly.

Key Management Activities

A description of 'Key Management Activities' as requested in the application can be presented in a timeline format. The timeline should address the major tasks areas and should cover a full year, beginning with the awarding of your grant. In the appropriate column, indicate *what* needs to happen and *who* will do it. Be specific! Some of the tasks listed below have many tasks within them that should be noted. A partial example follows.

What to Include In a Timeline

	Program Administration	Facility Development	Program Planning and Implementation	Program Evaluation	Staff Development
List each task in the month and quarter in which it will occur	All tasks and assignments related to: • hiring of start-up planner • recruitment and hiring of staff • budget revisions	All tasks and assignments related to: • negotiations for purchase or lease of space • construction or renovation of space • licensing of new or renovated facility • purchase of equipment, finishings, and supplies • classroom set up • required inspections	All tasks and assignments related to: • review of program requirements • finalizing prelminary inter-agency agreements • updating policies, procedures, forms to comply with HS/ESH guidelines • recruiting and enrolling families • arranging home visits • organizing and staffing Policy Council and other committees • conducting screenings for newly enrolled children	All tasks and assignments related to: • quarterly progress reports to Board of Directors, Policy Council, others • on-going data collection and analysis • planning for program adjustments in Year Two	All tasks and assignments related to: • training plans for speciic positions • staff development strategies • orientation plans for new staff • planning for attendance at conferences and workshops

Sample Timeline

	Program Administration	Facility Development	Program Planning and Implementation	Program Evaluation	Staff Development
Month Two (Quarter One)	Director, program manager, and social services manager attend national EHS orientation Program manager reviews applications for infant/toddler coordinator Human resources (HR) director schedules candidates for interviews	Negotiations on the purchase of proposed site are finalized by executive director, finance manager, and seller Construction bids are opened and contract selected by committee of board and staff	Program manager and social services manager: • revise enrollment materials to include EHS requirements • distribute family recruitment flyers to community agencies • finalize inter-agency agreements	Program manager completes summary of activities for Month Two	Program manager develops strategies for staff development and training
Month Three (Quarter One)	Program manager identifies final candidates for infant/toddler coordinator HR places ads for new positions HR holds a job fair to recruit for all other EHS positions	Construction company obtains permits for new facility	Program manager updates program policies, procedures, forms, and other written materials to meet EHS guidelines Social services manager meets with Part C programs to discuss implementation strategies	Program manager completes: • summary of activities for Month Three • quarterly report Program manager presents reports to Policy Council and Board of Directors	Program manager creates orientation plan for infant/toddler coordinator

Third Party Agreements

Here you are asked to specify the partnerships and linkages you will establish with other community agencies on behalf of Early Head Start families.

The key here is specificity.

What commitments are your partners willing to make? Are they contributing staff? Dollars? Facilities? What have they agreed to do? What have you agreed to do? You should be able to earn all of the available scoring points for this section if you:

1) identify all potential partners — not just who usually partners with you, but who is needed in terms of the services they provide;

2) define with each third party what specific services will be offered over what period of time. If the organization is unable to do so until a formal contract is signed, secure a statement of intent;

3) think 'out of the box' in describing other linkages with community resources — not just health, education, or social service agencies, but businesses, sports teams, retailers, media outlets, community service clubs, etc. Be creative and be specific.

Don't give up when the third party agreement letters fail to show up in the mail on or before the date you requested. If an organization has verbally agreed to partner with you, be persistent. Expect that you will have to hand-carry agreement letters to certain organizations and park yourself in their reception area in order to come away with signed agreements in time to meet your deadline.

It's a good idea to assign a 'runner' whose job it is — starting a week before the proposal has to leave your office — to collect inter-agency agreements and letters of support.

Sample Request for Inter-Agency Agreement

Date

Name
Title
Organization
Mailing Address
City, State, ZIP

Dear (**Addressee**):

(**Name of agency**) is requesting an Inter-Agency Agreement from you for its application to the Head Start Bureau of the Administration on Children, Youth, and Families. Our application will be for (**number**) families, including expectant mothers and children from birth to age 3 in (**program option**) in (**name of community**).

This proposed program will offer comprehensive services to some of the area's most vulnerable children and their families.

Please mail your signed Inter-Agency Agreement by (**date — no later than one week prior to proposal deadline**) to:

Name
Title
Agency
Mailing Address
City, State, ZIP

If you have any questions, please call me at (**direct dial number**). Thank you for your help.

Sincerely,

Name
Title

enclosure

Sample Statement of Intent
(Name of Your Agency)
Early Head Start
Inter-Agency Agreement

Statement of Intent

_____ agrees to collaborate/cooperate with (**name of agency**)'s Early Head Start Program and other service agencies/organizations that support it. We understand that this statement is an initial acknowledgement of our intent to participate in collaborative/cooperative efforts on behalf of Early Head Start clients. One of the ways we may support the project is by designating an Early Head Start Representative and encouraging our Representative to attend Early Head Start meetings.

We will abide by the Early Head Start mission statement and support the decisions of the Early Head Start Team. We recognize our cooperative purpose is to serve the physical, socio-emotional, cognitive, and environmental needs of eligible children in (**name of community**) from pre-natal through 3 years of age.

We understand that (**name of agency**) is requesting funds to serve (**number**) families in (**name of community**) with infants and toddlers, including expectant mothers in (**program option**) and agrees to:
1) provide referrals to our agency;
2) provide services to our eligible clients in their Early Head Start program, on a space available basis; if space is not available, they will assist our clients in finding similar services.

Since the well-being and development of the whole child is our major goal/concern, we will work collaboratively toward a community-wide approach to service delivery, which is easily accessible, affordable, minimizes duplication, maximizes resources, and meets the needs of children and their families.

On an annual basis, our organization will provide the following services:
- _____
- _____

It is our understanding that upon securing the Early Head Start grant, (**name of agency**) will provide a formal, comprehensive Inter-Agency Agreement outlining each entity's obligations.

_____	_____
Name (printed)	Title
_____	_____
Signature	Phone Number

_____
Date

Budget and Budget Justification

The budget section of a government grant application offers another opportunity to make the case for your program. This time, however, the case is not based on demonstrated need — it's based on *value*: what the program costs in relation to its expected outcomes. Weave the idea of value throughout this section, explaining costs and pointing out economies where they exist. Bear in mind that, while reviewers may frown on costs that they deem too high, they may also question costs that seem insufficient to accomplish the objectives.

Most of the errors in preparing this section arise from not following instructions — either omitting information, failing to provide a clear narrative that describes how the costs are derived, or inadequately justifying why a particular item is necessary or costs what it does.

As in the 'needs' section, data are essential. There are three kinds of data that can help you make the case for your funding request.

Benchmark data indicate whether your major costs (salaries, benefits, occupancy) are in line with the rest of the labor and leased space market in your area. That can be documented using published salary surveys, querying other employers, talking with real estate brokers, etc.

Analysis of your costs will allow you to determine and explain that it is more cost-effective to have a cook and fully-equipped kitchen at your site than to have meals catered.

Present your unit cost data — cost per child per attendance day, cost per enrollment day, perhaps even cost per hour. You can't tinker with the cost, but you can choose which data to present that will portray your program in the most favorable light.

The third kind of data you need is the *value of in-kind contributions*. If your program occupies free or reduced-cost space, make sure you know and report its fair-market value. Put a realistic dollar-value on all goods and services that you would otherwise have to pay for.

What is critical to demonstrate to proposal reviewers is not so much what your program costs, but the fact that you have a handle on what these costs are, and you can explain and justify them.

Cost is cost. If you ask for less money than you truly need, you may have to serve fewer children, operate fewer hours per week or months per year, or offer fewer services. If, instead, you start chipping away at program quality — trying to get by with fewer staff than you know you need, paying them less than a living wage, giving each child a quarter of an orange instead of a half — you run the risk of undermining all of the work you've put into submitting the grant application, to say nothing of the effort you've put into building your program.

That said, if your budget request exceeds the funding level allocated for this program in your state, you will have to make some adjustments.

Examples

Budget Justification
Benefits and Taxes — $182, 078

In addition to payroll taxes, the agency provides workers' compensation insurance, group medical insurance, long-term disability insurance, life insurance, and a retirement plan. Benefits costs are analyzed and services re-bid annually. The benefits package is competitive with those packages currently offered to the semi-skilled and skilled labor market in Maple City and is necessary for recruitment of qualified personnel.

Comprehensive benefits are provided; costs are reviewed annually, costs are benchmarked for this market

High Quality at a Reasonable Cost
The costs of operating our high-quality child care programs are offset by reduced staff turnover. Our annual staff turnover rate is 9%, compared to an industry-wide average approaching 40%. We have determined that our out-of-pocket cost of replacing one classroom staff member is $772 (advertising, medical and drug screening, background check, CPR and First Aid training). *Actual* cost, including human resources staff time, trainer's time, and intense supervision, brings

Detailed analysis of cost offsets

the total cost of each new hire to over $1,600.
We contract with various service providers in the
community at reduced rates for medical exams, dental
work, speech therapy, physical therapy, and related
services.

*Containing costs
while providing
needed services*

Staff Compensation

Our agency closely monitors compensation levels in
order to attract and retain qualified and effective staff.
Salaries are routinely benchmarked using a variety of
sources, including the Community Council of Greater
Maple City's Non-Profit Salary Survey. This survey is
distributed every three years; the latest data were
gathered last year and include positions specific to
early childhood programs.

*Salary scales are set
based on surveys of
market rates for
like positions*

We also use the Maple City Standard Metropolitan
Statistical Area prepared by the State Employment
Commission and data from the National Center for the
Early Childhood Work Force. Our salary scale is adjusted
when market conditions so warrant. Early Head Start
COLAs, as they are made available, will be applied to
wages as market adjustments.

Staff Development and Training

In addition to funds set aside for staff attendance at
appropriate workshops and conferences, we offer an
Educational Assistance Program that reimburses staff for
a portion of their tuition and fees for related college
courses.

*There are specific
funds allocated and
a plan for their
distribution*

Staff are also rewarded for educational attainment.
Those who earn their CDA credentials receive a $250
annual stipend. Those who attain AA degrees have their
annual salaries increased by $1,000. Staff who earn
Bachelor's degrees are paid an additional $1,500 per
year.

Appendices

The appendices are where you will place requested documents (maps, job
descriptions, organization charts, letters of support, etc.), along with other
documents that enhance your proposal (relevant newspaper articles, etc.).

Each appendix that is referenced in the proposal narrative (*an organization chart is attached as Appendix I*) should be labeled. Similar documents (letters of support or job descriptions) can be grouped within a single appendix, as long as all items are related. Where there are multiple documents in a single appendix, type a cover page that lists the contents of that appendix:

Appendix II

Job Descriptions

Health Services Specialist
Infant/Toddler Coordinator
Inclusion Specialist
Infant/Toddler Teacher

Key program positions include the program's management staff plus everyone who works directly with children and/or families. Be sure that any qualifications you stipulate in the proposal narrative are reflected in the job description.

Job descriptions should be included for 1) the key program positions that are vacant and, thus, whose significance cannot be evaluated by the resumé of the person holding the job, or 2) a job held by multiple individuals (e.g., teacher).

If you are submitting hard copies of a map originally printed in color, make color copies. Although what the reviewers look at may be second generation, black and white copies of what you have submitted, the review panel is not likely to study the map closely. The members of the panel are not from your area, so the program location will have little meaning to them. It does have meaning, however, for the Head Start Bureau personnel who define the boundaries of the service areas in which funding will be offered, so you want to make sure that they have the clearest view.

Letters of Support

When you ask an individual to prepare a letter of support, assume that person will ask for specific information to incorporate into the letter or request a sample of what you expect. Often, you will be asked to write the letter for his/her signature.

If the person is willing to write an 'original' letter, provide a bulleted list of facts — the name of the funding source to whom to address the letter, the name of the grant or program, a brief description of what you are proposing, the amount you are requesting, plus any other critical information.

If the individual asks you to provide a sample letter, do so — but be aware that each letter you prepare will have to be different; otherwise, the reviewers will quickly notice the identical letters and surmise that they were not written by the signers.

Although letters of support can be collated alphabetically, they have more impact when they are organized according to their significance to the program and/or the prominence of the individual writing/signing the letter.

For example:

- United States Senator

- Mayor

- Head Start Policy Council Chair

- United Way Executive

- Local Workforce Development Board Chair

- ECI/Part C Program Director

- Chamber of Commerce Executive

- Business Leader(s)

- Service Organization (Kiwanis, Junior League, etc.) President

- Local/Regional Office of State Child Care Licensing Agency Manager

- Professional Association President

- Other Community Agencies (*not* those with whom you will have Inter-Agency Agreements).

Sample Request for Letter of Support

Date

Name
Title
Organization
Mailing Address
City, State, ZIP

Dear (**Addressee**):

(**Name of agency**) is requesting a letter of support from you for its application to the Head Start Bureau of the Administration on Children, Youth and Families. (**As applicable**): We appreciate your willingness to express your support for our application last year/in previous years. Although our applications have not been funded, we are trying again, because of the need in our community. (**Or**)
Your letter of support added immeasurably to our successful application.

We are requesting funds to serve (**number**) families with infants and toddlers, including expectant mothers, in (**program option**) in (**name of community**).

The new program will offer comprehensive services to some of the area's most vulnerable children and their families. We have been providing Head Start services in (**name of community**) since (**year**). Early Head Start services, however, are not now available there.

Please address your letter of support to: **Name and Title**
                                             Agency
                                             Mailing Address
                                             City, State, ZIP

Please mail your letter to the attention of (**person at your agency**) at (**your agency address**) by (**date — no later than one week prior to proposal deadline**). If you have any questions, call (**person at your agency**) at (**direct dial number**).

(**As applicable**): A copy of the letter you wrote last year is attached for your reference.

Again, thank you for your help.

Sincerely,

Name
Title

enclosure

This is a **sample** of a sample: an example of a letter sent to a local business leader to serve as a template for his letter of support for your proposed program

(Use this heading)

Sample Letter of Support On Your Letterhead

Date

Name of Applicant Agency Director
Title
Agency
Mailing Address
City, State, ZIP

Dear (**Addressee**):

As a member of the (**name of city**) business community, who is concerned about the provision of high-quality child development services for the young children who are our city's future, I commend and support (**name of agency**)'s proposal to offer Early Head Start services.

Your model of (**program option**) addresses the importance of consistent, nurturing caregivers to the healthy emotional and intellectual development of children. It's an approach I admire and support.

I wish you much success and endorse your efforts on behalf of the children of our community.

Sincerely,

Name
Title

Sample Tracking Form for Letters of Support

Requested From	Request Sent	Need Pick-Up?	Received	Thank You Sent	Contact Informed of Results
(agency/contact)	(date)	(yes/no)	(date)	(date)	(date)

CHAPTER 8

Breaking New Ground: The Capital Campaign

A capital campaign is just what the name implies — a time-limited initiative (perhaps two or three years for an early childhood organization) to raise money to acquire or improve a physical asset. It's a 'campaign' in the sense that it involves pre-planning, specific stages, and the allocation of financial and human resources, including a pool of new and committed volunteers. You could conduct a capital campaign to purchase land for eventual expansion, to construct or buy a new building, to renovate your existing facility, to equip your playground, or for any purpose related to a physical asset.

Since a capital campaign involves a significant amount of work, it should be undertaken only if you need to raise a significant amount of money. If you 'just' need a new roof or furnace or an additional outdoor climbing structure, try to raise the money by increasing your annual fundraising goal or by a few well-researched requests to specific funders.

Even though your campaign goal will be considerably greater than your annual fundraising goal, take heart from the fact that it is almost always easier to raise money for capital needs than for program costs. There are two primary reasons. One, donors understand 'bricks and mortar.' They can see where their dollars are going. A building or playground is visible, tangible proof of their generosity. Of course donors understand that your program couldn't keep the doors open without funds for salaries; but there's a difference between admiring a beautiful, new classroom and saying to oneself, "My money helped build this," and observing the teachers at work and wondering, "which person's salary am I helping to pay?"

Second, capital campaigns offer a variety of naming opportunities. The building, the preschool wing, an infant room, the kitchen, the teachers' break room, the reception area, the adult restroom, the parent library (even if it consists of a book shelf), the director's office, the playground (or specific play areas), the outdoor entry, and any piece of equipment that will hold a plaque with the donor's name on it can be presented to potential contributors as a way of recognizing their gift. Be creative! Just remember to align the naming opportunity with the size of the contribution. If a donor wishes to remain anonymous, honor that request . . . and 'sell' that naming opportunity to another prospect.

How Much Money Will You Need?

If you are planning to build or renovate a facility, you should be working with an architect, project manager, or contractor who can give you a realistic idea of how much the project will cost. These costs are likely to include some or all of the following:

- land purchase

- site work (grading, sewer and water line connections, paving, etc.)

- permits, fees, bonds, insurance

- construction materials (steel, lumber, concrete, roofing, etc.)

- carpentry (framing, finish, millwork, etc.)

- drywall and metal studs

- windows and doors (including window coverings)

- ceiling finish

- flooring (tile, carpeting, etc.)

- plumbing (including sprinkler system)

- wall finishes (paint, wall coverings)

- heating, ventilating, and air conditioning

- electrical (indoor and outdoor lighting, computer networking, etc.)

- off-street parking and driveway(s)

- landscaping

- fencing

- security features (wiring, keypads, etc.)

- playground design, construction, and paving

- professional fees (architect, interior design, landscape design, legal, engineering — mechanical, civil, structural, environmental, soil)

- contingency (usually 10-15% of estimated total expense)

In addition to these estimates, you will need to create a budget for furnishings, equipment, and supplies — classroom furniture and equipment, office furniture and equipment, food service equipment and supplies, furnishings for adult areas (reception, work rooms, etc.).

Finally, add the costs of the campaign itself. You may want to hire a consultant — an individual or firm to assist with the planning and implementation of the campaign. You'll need to cover the costs of printing your case statement. You'll need additional stationery and postage, refreshments for campaign committee meetings, donor recognition plaques, and dollars for special events (ground-breaking, donor recognition activities, ribbon-cutting, etc.).

All of these expenses should be reflected in your capital campaign goal. If you are building or renovating a facility, consider adding a maintenance endowment to the overall goal to provide the money in future years for capital improvements. A maintenance endowment is not intended to pay 'routine' maintenance costs that should be included in your annual operating budget (lawn mowing, snow removal, furnace filters, air conditioning service, plumbing repairs). Instead, it is for the purpose of replacing roofs, furnaces, floor coverings, appliances, and other items that eventually show the wear and tear of daily use or for improvements that were unforeseen at the time of the building's original construction, but are later found to be necessary. The funds for these expenses will come from the interest earned by the endowment, not the principal. Thus, it's important for your board of directors to identify an appropriate investment vehicle which can be described to prospective donors as part of the overall campaign information.

Where Will the Money Come From?

Organizations embarking on capital campaigns typically create a gift range chart which shows how many gifts of what size are required to meet their goal. Usually, 40-60% of the goal will come from a handful of donors — six to eight at most. So, if you want to raise $2 million your chart might look like this:

Number of Gifts	Size	Range Total	Cumulative Total
1	$400,000	$400,000	$ 400,000
2	$200,000	$400,000	$ 800,000
4	$100,000	$400,000	$1,200,000

The remaining $800,000 will come from a larger number of donors, giving in smaller amounts.

5	$40,000	$200,000	$1,400,000
10	$20,000	$200,000	$1,600,000
20	$10,000	$200,000	$1,800,000
50	$ 2,000	$100,000	$1,900,000
100	$ 1,000	$100,000	$2,000,000

Clearly, the key to a successful $2 million campaign is to identify the sources of the first $1.2 million. Once that money is secured, it will be much easier to find the rest. Bear in mind that not every source you approach will make a contribution, and those who do may not give what you requested. So, for the one $400,000 contribution you need, try to target at least four prospects. Similarly, for the two $200,000 gifts, identify eight to 10 sources. Look for 16-20 prospects who could each make a $100,000 gift.

As you go down the chart, you can get by with a lower ratio of prospects to donors, because the gifts of those whom you had asked at higher levels, but who made smaller contributions than you requested, will make up part of the lower levels.

The Capital Campaign Committee

Since you will be relying on large gifts to insure the success of your campaign, you will need a campaign committee drawn from the people in your community who can give and get such amounts, chaired by a 'big name.' This is not a member of your board of directors. Rather, it is a community leader who will serve as the 'spokesperson' for the campaign (even though you will probably supply the words); who will make calls (personal or telephone) on colleagues and friends to ask for money; who will speak before church and civic groups; and who will himself or herself make a lead gift.

As noted in Chapter 1, anyone who asks someone else for a contribution must have already made his or her own gift — either personally or from corporate coffers. Because this is for a special purpose, it should be significantly larger than the person's usual contribution, assuming she or he has already given to your organization. If it is a first-time gift, it should be a 'capacity' gift — reflecting what the donor is *able* to give, not merely *willing* to give.

The more money you receive up front from the capital campaign committee, the easier it will be to persuade other prospects to make sizeable gifts — and the less you will have to raise from other sources.

Use your board members to recruit the campaign leadership. Again, you should already have people on your board who have the kind of relationships with business and civic leaders that will enable them to identify a potential campaign chair, persuade the candidate of the value of your organization, convince the person of the need for the campaign, and announce the happy news to the rest of the board. If you don't have that resource, defer your capital campaign until you do. You don't want to risk launching a campaign that fails for lack of appropriate leadership.

The campaign committee members also solicit funds — from individuals whom they know personally or companies with whom they have business relationships. They plan donor-recognition activities and special events. They review drafts of campaign literature, including the case statement. They sign off on recommended gift amounts for specific naming opportunities. They approve the campaign budget. They have a huge and important role that deserves special and continuing recognition.

Preparing the Committee for its Work

If you are lucky, your organization will be able to identify individuals for membership on the capital campaign committee who have served in the same capacity with other organizations. They are experienced at, and comfortable with, asking people of means to make large gifts. If that's not the case, the committee members will need some training. Your organization has only one chance with each major prospect — you want the committee member making the solicitation to be fully prepared when he or she makes the request. Find a fundraising expert in your community to work with the committee for at least a half-day session. If the individual will donate his or her time, that's wonderful. Otherwise, plan to pay the requested fee. If your community has a chapter of the Association of Fundraising Professionals, start there. Or contact your local United Way for a referral. Typically, the training will cover the basic concepts of fundraising, specific techniques for major gift solicitation, dealing with prospects' concerns and objections, and role-playing exercises.

Once the training has been completed, provide the committee with specific instructions and materials. Every member will need information about each prospect on his or her list: name, contact information, the prospect's relationship to the organization, the prospect's special interests, and the amount to request.

The amount to request is generally based on the committee's assessment of the prospect's capacity to give, along with a review of the prospect's history with the organization (especially previous gifts), and gifts given to other organizations. The relationship of the solicitor to the prospect is also a factor to be considered. There's more than a little truth to the so-called 'foolproof' method of raising money: write the most compelling letter you can and sign it with the addressee's mother's name.

Committee members should have a printed log or access to a database for recording each contact, including progress to date, comments, and the outcome. They will need a calendar of key dates — by when they should complete their initial contacts, calls, and follow-ups, as well as reporting dates and committee meeting times. They will need a supply of campaign stationery, although it is acceptable (and often preferable) to use their own personal or corporate letterhead.

The Case Statement

The other major resource the committee members will need is a well-thought-out, attractively-presented case statement. This is the document that makes the case for the campaign: who your organization is, what you are planning to do with the money, how the project will make a difference to the people you serve, how the prospect can make a contribution, and how donors will be recognized.

The case statement is like an investment prospectus. It explains why the prospect's gift is a good investment — not only why your organization needs financial support, but also why you merit it. A well-written case statement, even though it ultimately makes the case for a capital contribution, can become the basis for all of your fundraising efforts. It tells the story of your organization — a story that can be excerpted, re-formatted, or used as the source of key messages in a variety of proposals, brochures, program descriptions, and other materials.

The capital campaign case statement will be several pages in length. It should cover your mission, your history of accomplishments, your programs, your governance, your distinctive competencies, the need the capital campaign will address, the specifics of the project (including architectural renderings, floor plans, etc.), project funding commitments to date (if none yet, list sources of your program funding), information on how the prospect can make the gift (over what timeframe, by what payment method, etc.), and naming opportunities. It should show your board of directors, with affiliations — perhaps on the inside of the front or back cover.

Have the document professionally designed and printed. Although early childhood programs typically don't have the resources of the museums, hospitals, or universities who are also seeking major gifts, you will be competing with them for the prospects' attention. Your case statement has to be on par with theirs. Play to your strength — the natural appeal of young children. Work with your graphics design expert to incorporate photographs of the children who benefit from your programs. If you can find a firm that will provide pro bono services, you will save some money. However, don't skimp on the case statement. Be prepared to pay for good design and printing on high-quality paper.

Since the case statement is a 'leave behind' for the prospect to examine in detail, prepare a one-page, bulleted fact sheet for the solicitor to talk from that summarizes the key points: your agency's mission and accomplishments, the need for the project, what you are proposing, and the campaign goal. You could also prepare a one-page list of naming opportunities. Any separate pages such as these should be inserted into a folder that includes the larger case statement.

When you prepare the case statement, think of what to say that will motivate the prospect to give. Despite being 'pretty,' many case statements tend to follow a lackluster format, telling: *who we are, what we do, what we need, where to send your check.*

Your case statement should aim to engage the prospect: *Eighty percent of the premature infants born in our community are born to teen mothers. These babies are at risk for learning problems when they get to school. If we don't help them get off to the best possible start during their earliest years, they are more likely to experience school failure and demonstrate behavior problems — eventually dropping out. This is our plan to prevent that unhappy outcome, who is already helping us; won't you join them in making a difference for our community's youngest, most vulnerable children?*

Case statements can include historical narrative:

> The Northside Child Care Agency was founded over 110 years ago by a group of wealthy women in Central City who were concerned about the plight of the children whose mothers worked in the city's cotton mills. Many of these children were left home alone while their mothers worked, or they were cared for by older siblings kept home from school to watch their brothers and sisters. The founders were determined to improve these conditions and 'passed the hat' among their family members and friends until enough money could be raised to buy a vacant house near the intersection of Third and Main Streets, purchase needed equipment and supplies, and hire Miss Catherine Ames as the organization's first Executive Director. The founders could not have envisioned how their early efforts would influence generations of children to come.

The case statement may also include an anecdote that introduces the need:

> Every morning, rain or shine, three-year-old Amelia and her mother walk the five blocks from their tiny apartment in North Central City to the Northside Child Development Center. Amelia has been on the center's waiting list for the past eight months. Her family cannot afford a telephone and Amelia's mother does not want to risk missing the opportunity to enroll her when the first opening occurs. So each day, the two of them visit the center to see if there is room for Amelia.

The Campaign Timetable

Capital campaigns are usually divided into the 'quiet' phase and the 'public' phase. During the quiet phase, the lead gifts (the first 50-60% of the amount needed) are solicited and secured. It can take up to a year or more, depending on the size of your campaign goal, to complete this phase. Often, a prospect will want to see how the campaign is progressing before making a commitment. It's not unusual for someone to say, *Come back to see me when you've raised the first $500,000.* Or you may encounter a prospect who makes a lesser gift at the beginning of the campaign, but will make a larger gift as the campaign rolls toward completion. The timeline is another reason for having a well-selected committee in place — their own contributions and their access to individuals who are able to make large gifts can jumpstart your quiet phase, significantly reducing the time until you can 'go public' to solicit a larger pool of prospects.

When the campaign is ready to go public, it does so with an event — either a groundbreaking or a celebration honoring the donors, prospects, committee, and the board. It's a good idea to invite the print and broadcast media — to give the project additional credibility, to announce to the public at large that you have already achieved 55% of your goal, and to stimulate interest among prospects who have yet to be solicited.

A groundbreaking is particularly appropriate if you can involve children. Televised or photographic images of children wearing little hard hats and digging with child-size shovels go a long way toward evoking an emotional response on the part of current and potential donors. Obviously, other arrangements will have to be made if there are safety issues at an undeveloped site, but to the extent that children can actively participate (even if your program does not serve children directly), you are making the best use of your own 'natural resources.'

Breaking ground with hand-held shovels does not commit your organization to begin construction. However, while the least risky approach is to start construction only after all of the money is raised, there are advantages to starting construction once the public phase of the campaign is launched. If you do so, prospects can see that the project is 'real' and that their money will be used immediately or in the very near future, rather than at some date months away. Your campaign committee members have a place to bring prospects and to show them exactly where the room with their name on it will be located (*see how the morning sun will shine in* or *this area will look out on the stand of pine trees on the hill*). You can walk those who have already given through the site (be sure to provide hard hats), as a courtesy or as a prelude to an additional request. This is especially helpful if there have been cost overruns that are outside of your organization's control (an unexpected increase in raw material prices or transportation costs) resulting in your original goal being too low to complete the project.

Your campaign ends, hopefully within the timeframe announced at its start, when all the money has been raised. If that occurs before the projected end date, stop there — even if there are other prospects to be solicited or requests are still outstanding. Announce your success with a celebration honoring everyone who had a role in achieving the goal. If your achievement does not motivate those prospects who have been solicited to send in their money, keep them on your prospect list for a future request.

What if you reach the campaign's announced end date and have not raised all the money required? You need to stop in that case as well. If it's not possible to make any changes to the project to fall in line with the available dollars, consider taking a mortgage for the remainder of the cost. You don't want to embarrass your committee members and board by extending the campaign.

CHAPTER 9

Writing to Win

Once you have written a funding proposal, give it to several people to read, and listen carefully to their suggestions. It's very helpful to have someone read it who is not familiar with your work. If that person gains a clear understanding of what your organization does, what need you meet, why additional funds are required, and how the dollars will be spent, you've done a good job.

Be willing to re-write. One of the common reasons to do some re-writing is to stay within the page limits stipulated by the funder. As you work on your proposal, write what you think you ought to say — then see if it fits. If it doesn't, start with the easy fixes. Unless the funder has specified font size or margins (government agencies often do, private funders usually don't), downsize the font a point or two or change to a smaller font. Since you want the words that you've toiled over to be read, be sure the font is not too small. If necessary, widen the margins slightly. Again, you don't want the document to look like you've spilled words all over the page, so be careful. You can usually manage a slightly shorter margin at the bottom of the page without anyone noticing.

If these solutions don't bring you within the page limits, take out your mental scalpel and start cutting. Work on using the fewest words possible to convey an idea. This is harder than it sounds — especially when you're writing to convince the reader to give you money. More words seem more persuasive. But *here's why* is simpler and shorter than saying *here's the reason to do so*. Even if you have plenty of space, when you write a sentence, look at it to see if phrases can be shortened without changing the meaning.

Avoid jargon and acronyms, especially if you are applying to a foundation, corporation, or individual who is not familiar with early childhood terminology. If you want to abbreviate a term that you are going to use more than once in the proposal, such as *National Association for the Education of Young Children*, spell it out the first time you use it, followed by its abbreviation in parentheses (*NAEYC*). You can then use the abbreviation throughout the rest of the document; although, to be safe, you should spell out the term the first time it appears in sections that might be read separately, such as the cover letter or proposal summary.

Further, don't assume that anyone reading your proposal knows what NAEYC is. Provide a brief explanation: *the largest professional membership organization in the early childhood field.*

Try to maintain consistency in usage. If your proposal refers to your organization in the third person — 'it,' do so throughout. *It is the oldest child development center in the city.* You might prefer the more personal 'we.' *We are the Child and Adult Care Food Program sponsor for more than 200 family child care providers.* Whichever form you like, use it consistently.

If you refer to 'parents' or 'families,' use 'children' and 'their.' It is incorrect to say, *Our goal is to help the parent educate their child.* The word 'parent' is singular — therefore the pronoun that follows must also be singular. *Our goal is to help the parent educate his or her child.* Or, *Our goal is to help parents educate their children.*

Although it's not always possible, try to write in the active voice. Doing so gives your proposal more energy — it suggests that your organization is active and vital, not passive and inert. One way to get in the habit of writing in the active voice is to go over what you've written each day — e-mails, memos, letters, reports, etc., to see how many passive-voice sentences you find. Then practice re-writing them in the active voice.

Here are some examples — taken from actual proposals — to start with:

Each component of our strategic plan will be evaluated quantitatively and qualitatively.

_____

_____

Attendance will be taken at each session and attendance records will be provided to the Department of Social Services.

_____

_____

The target population will be recruited to fill entry-level jobs created by the proposed program.

_____

_____

Many proposals require the reviewer to wade through formal, stilted, and redundant language. That's understandable — the writer is trying to demonstrate the organization's professionalism, the importance of its work, and the seriousness of the need. But long and convoluted sentences are not usually persuasive. Wordiness does not indicate worthiness. And poor grammar reflects poorly on the organization.

Try your hand at re-writing these actual drafts of proposal language. Suggested revisions follow (no peeking — you can probably do as well or better).

We live in an era in which a series of technological explosions have resulted in the availability of more specific data and information about human development than ever available before. What we knew about infant brain development in the past, for example, we learned in a variety of different ways: autopsies, anecdotal records regarding atypical development, and the like. Today, thanks to positive emission tomography, we can view the actual functioning of the healthy infant brain through non-invasive imaging technology.

_____

_____

_____

_____

Our agency primarily serves low-income families, where they are confronted by many problems, chief among them are finding employment and providing the basic necessities of life, like a home and food for their children. Our program design offers care for infants and toddlers in family child care and care for preschoolers in centers.

_____

_____

_____

_____

Today's business environment relies on the maximum productivity of its workforce. It is more important than ever to be able to attract and retain productive employees in order to stay competitive in their market. Child care problems can adversely affect the job performance of employees.

_____
_____
_____
_____

A summer program assistant will need to be hired. Hiring qualifications include previous experience with working for a summer program, completion of or currently being enrolled in a four-year degree program, passing drug and criminal background check screenings, certification in CPR and First Aid, and meeting all state licensing standards.

_____
_____
_____
_____

Revisions

As originally written:

> We live in an era in which a *series of technological explosions* have resulted in the *availability* of more specific *data and information* about human development than ever *available* before. What we knew about infant brain development in the past, for example, we learned in a *variety of different ways*: *autopsies*, anecdotal records regarding atypical development, and the like. Today, thanks to *positive emission tomography*, we can view the actual functioning of the healthy infant brain through *non-invasive imaging technology*.

Comments:

- *a series of technological explosions* sounds like a disaster in the high-tech industry

- *availability* and *available* are repetitive

- *data* and *information* are redundant

- *a variety of different ways* is also redundant: *a variety of ways* or *different ways*

- *autopsies* present an unfortunate image in a proposal relating to infant brain development

- *positive emission tomography* **is** *non-invasive imaging technology.*

Suggested revision:

> New imaging technology has enabled researchers to better understand infant brain development.

As originally written:

> Our agency primarily serves low-income families, *where* they are confronted by *many problems, chief among them* are finding employment and providing the basic *necessities of life, like a home and food* for their children. *Our program design* offers care for infants and toddlers in family child care and care for preschoolers in centers.

Comments:

- *where* is a term related to location

- *many problems, chief among them* is a run-on phrase that should be broken into two sentences (. . . *many problems. Chief among them. . .*)

- *necessities of life, like a home and food* is redundant, rather than explanatory

- *our program design* should begin a new paragraph.

Suggested revision:

> Our agency serves primarily low-income families. The availability of high-quality child care is essential to their ability to become self-sufficient.
>
> *Our program design* offers care for infants and toddlers in family child care and care for preschoolers in centers.

As originally written:

> Today's business environment relies on the maximum productivity of its workforce. It is more important than ever to be able to attract and retain productive employees in order to stay competitive in *their* market. Child care problems can adversely affect the job performance of employees.

Comments:

- *their* should be replaced with *the*

- there is nothing 'technically' wrong with this statement, but it lacks punch

Suggested revision:

> Employers depend on employees who depend on child care in order to work.

As originally written:

> A summer program assistant *will need to be* hired. *Hiring* qualifications include previous experience *with* working for a summer program, completion of or *is currently enrolled* in a four-year degree program, *passes drug and criminal background check screenings, certification in CPR and First Aid, and meets all state licensing standards.*

Comments:

- *will need to be hired* can be shortened to *will be hired*

- *hiring* qualifications is redundant

- *with* is unnecessary

- *is currently enrolled* should be changed to *current enrollment*

- *passes drug and criminal background check screenings, certification in CPR and First Aid, and meets all state licensing standards* can be shortened to *compliance with all licensing standards.*

Suggested revision:

A summer program assistant will be hired. Qualifications include previous employment in a summer program, completion of or current enrollment in a four-year degree program, and compliance with state licensing requirements.

CHAPTER 10

Where to Find Help

An Internet search, using the words 'grantwriting' or 'fundraising' will lead you into a vast universe of resources — some free, some for sale; some reputable, some less so.

As a general rule, trust organizations that have a history of providing the information you are seeking — those that have earned a reputation for excellence among funders and fundraising professionals. That is not to suggest that smaller, newer entities, or even individuals, cannot provide help that will be invaluable. It's just that they may be harder to identify and the quality of their services more difficult to verify.

Many universities offer proposal writing courses or online libraries of articles on grantwriting, tips, and/or sample proposals. These offerings will appear on lists generated by Internet search engines, although you'll have to scroll to find them, or you can search your state's universities' web sites. If your states' schools don't offer these resources, try other states.

If you are seeking corporate funding and have identified some prospects, such as those suggested in Chapter 5, go directly to each company's web site. You'll find information on their grantmaking when you click past the homepage that opens with the company's products or services. For example, to learn about Toyota's grantmaking, click on *About Toyota* (at the top of the screen), then *Our Company*, then *Our Commitment*, then *Philanthropy*, then *Education*, and, finally, *Grants*. On AT&T's homepage, click on *About Us*, followed by *Company Information*, *Corporate Social Responsibility*, *Corporate Giving*, and *AT&T Foundation*. At UPS, click on *About UPS*, *UPS and the Community*, *Philanthropy*, and *Grant Guidelines*. Each company's web site will be slightly different, but the information is always there if you dig for it.

The best source of information on the world of foundations is the Foundation Center. This organization, founded in 1956, offers a print directory of foundations, a searchable CD-ROM, and an online directory. The electronic directories allow you to search foundations by location (city or state) and by field of interest (children, education, women, etc.), along with other criteria. If you are in an area where there are no foundations, you can search by grantees. What organizations in your area or state have received funding from foundations located elsewhere? The information on the foundations includes examples of grants, dollar range of grants, and names of trustees. The Center also publishes a number of other directories related to philanthropy, as well as guidebooks and manuals. If you don't wish to subscribe to the Foundation Center's services, find out if your local library system does. In addition to its publications, the Center offers workshops on fundraising, grantseeking, proposal writing, and related topics at locations around the country. The Foundation Center's web site is **www.FdnCenter.org**. Its phone number is (800) 424-9386; the mailing address is 79 Fifth Avenue, New York, NY 10003-3076.

If you already know of certain foundations, either in or outside of your area, use an Internet search engine to go directly to their web sites. There you will find information about the foundations' missions, areas of interest, funding policies, boards of trustees, and previous grantees. You will also learn how to apply, using the guidelines provided and/or online application forms. While it's tempting to link directly to the application guidelines or forms, take the time to read whatever the site says about the foundation itself: its mission, history, founders, policies, etc. This information can give you valuable insight into what you should emphasize in your request and it can provide verbiage that you might want to reflect in your proposal.

Another excellent resource is the Grantsmanship Center[SM], founded in 1972. This organization conducts grantwriting workshops across the country, publishes a widely-read, proposal-writing guide, as well as a periodical, posts daily grant announcements on its web site, and maintains online databases of government, foundation, and corporate funding sources. The Grantsmanship Center's web site is **www.TGCI.com**. Its phone number is (213) 482-9860; the mailing address is PO Box 17220, Los Angeles, CA 90017.

Information on federal government grants can be found at **www.Grants.gov**. This site works best if you have seen or heard about a particular grant announcement. You can use the Funding Opportunity Number (FON) or Catalog of Federal Domestic

Assistance (CFDA) number, both of which are included in the announcement, or keyword to search for the grant application. If you are simply browsing for opportunities, you can search by keywords or browse the list of agencies offering grant opportunities, but you are likely to generate a lengthy list, most of which won't be of interest.

If you have heard about a federal funding opportunity, but can't find any information on it (you don't have Internet access or time to search), contact the office of your member of Congress. Someone on the staff (probably in the D.C. office) should be able to get the information you need by calling the agency that has posted the announcement. Remember to send a written thank-you note, along with the message that you would welcome a letter of support from the member.

Announcements of state grants are found on the appropriate state agency's web site. Some sites are more user-friendly than others, with visible links to funding opportunities, but they all post these announcements somewhere. If the agency offers a way to sign up to be notified when grants become available, make sure you do so. It's wise to sign up with or at least regularly visit the web site of any state agency whose funds might support some aspect of your organization — human services, health, education, juvenile justice, employment, community development, etc.

Professional membership organizations at the national, state, and local levels can be good sources of information about funding opportunities if their publications or web site postings are current. Often, by the time the members are notified of the opportunity, the application deadline is at hand or has passed. For that reason, it's safest to do your own research. If you are an active member of an organization that has the potential to notify its members of the availability of grants, but does not have the current capacity to get the job done, bring the issue up at a board or membership meeting, or even better, volunteer to work with another member to do it. Don't worry about widening the pool of applicants — the cream will rise to the top — and *you've* had the advantage of reading this book!

CHAPTER 11

Summing Up

Whether your program is supported primarily by parent fees, child care voucher payments, donations, or grants, your finances will be more stable, and your board and staff will enjoy more peace of mind if you have diverse sources of support that grow out of a fund development plan appropriate for your organization. Diversification helps protect your budget when one funding source is reduced or disappears altogether. That, alone, is reason enough to aim for a realistic plan that includes public and private sources, multi-year grants or contracts, annual appeals, and signature events.

This book has described the *who, what, why, when,* and *how* of strengthening your funding base. The main ideas are summarized in the following list. Use them to guide your planning and to measure your results.

1. Keep *children at the heart* of any funding request you make — whether it is funds for a new roof, a staff training program, or a parent library.

2. Recruit and nurture *the right leadership.* Staff cannot raise money alone. The active participation of volunteers who represent the community is crucial.

3. Work with your board and staff to identify a base of potential donors and *build and maintain relationships* with them — in person, via direct mail, and online.

4. Consider the *effort* and the *likely effectiveness* of various fund development activities. Your organization's capacity is a key determinant of success.

5. *Do your homework* before applying for a grant. Targeting the appropriate funding source with a solid proposal saves a lot of disappointment down the road.

6. Create a *well-written case statement* to serve as the basis of all your fundraising materials — proposals, brochures, program descriptions, annual requests, etc.

7. *Rely on resources* that are easily accessible. Don't waste time digging for information that's already available on the Internet or from one of the organizations whose purpose is to help agencies be more effective in securing funds.

A Final Word

Raising money can seem like a daunting task. Few people, other than those who have chosen this profession, like to do it. It's hard work and carries the risk of rejection. For individuals who have committed their careers to helping children and families, asking for money (whether crafting a proposal, selling tickets to a luncheon, or writing letters) can feel, at best, like a time-consuming distraction that takes you away from your 'real' work and, at worst, that you're no different than someone selling aluminum siding.

But who else has the passion that will move a potential donor to write a check? Who else has the profound understanding of young children's needs that can be translated into a program plan to be presented to a major funding source? Who else can escort a corporate executive or a public policymaker on a tour of a child development center and point out how the program is preparing the children for school?

The Chinese philosopher Lao Tzu said that a journey of a thousand miles starts with a single step. Yours is a journey of dollars, not miles, but his ancient wisdom applies nonetheless. Start with the first step — in this case, making a plan. Then take the next step, and the next, and the one after that. Celebrate your successes, no matter how small. And keep in mind, small successes lead to big ones!